Danish Food & Cooking

Traditions · Ingredients · Tastes · Techniques · 65 Classic Recipes

Danish Food & Cooking

Judith H Dern

Consultant: John Nielsen

with photographs by William Lingwood

aquamarine

This edition is published by Aquamarine, an imprint of Anness Publishing Ltd, Blaby Road, Wigston, Leicestershire LE18 4SE

Email: info@anness.com

Web: www.aquamarinebooks.com; www.annesspublishing.com

If you like the images in this book and would like to investigate using them for publishing, promotions or advertising, please visit our website www.practicalpictures.com for more information.

Publisher: Joanna Lorenz
Editorial Director: Helen Sudell
Executive Editor: Joanne Rippin
Designer: Simon Daley
Photography: William Lingwood
Food Stylist: Fergal Connolly
Prop Stylist: Helen Trent
Senior Production Controller: Claire Rae

Ethical trading policy

Because of our ongoing ecological investment programme, you, as our customer, can have the pleasure and reassurance of knowing that a tree is being cultivated on your behalf to naturally replace the materials used to make the book you are holding. For further information about this scheme, go to www.annesspublishing.com/trees.

Publisher's Note

Although the advice and information in this book are believed to be accurate and true at the time of going to press, neither the authors nor the publisher can accept any legal responsibility or liability for any errors or omissions that may have been made nor for any inaccuracies nor for any loss, harm or injury that comes about from following instructions or advice in this book.

Notes

Bracketed terms are intended for American readers. For all recipes, quantities are given in both metric and imperial measures and, where appropriate, in standard cups and spoons. Follow one set of measures, but not a mixture, because they are not interchangeable.

Standard spoon and cup measures are level. 1 tsp = 5ml, 1 tbsp = 15ml, 1 cup = 250ml/8fl oz.

Australian standard tablespoons are 20ml. Australian readers should use 3 tsp in place of 1 tbsp for measuring small quantities.

American pints are 16fl oz/2 cups. American readers should use 20fl oz/2.5 cups in place of 1 pint when measuring liquids.

Electric oven temperatures in this book are for conventional ovens. When using a fan oven, the temperature will probably need to be reduced by about 10–20°C/20–40°F. Since ovens vary, you should check with your manufacturer's instruction book for more guidance.

The nutritional analysis given for each recipe is calculated per portion (i.e. serving or item), unless otherwise stated. If the recipe gives a range, such as Serves 4–6, then the nutritional analysis will be for the smaller portion size. The analysis does not include optional ingredients, such as salt added to taste.

Medium (US large) eggs are used unless otherwise stated.

Front cover shows Roast Pork with Crackling and Glazed Potatoes – for recipe, see page 80.

Contents

Introduction   6

Appetizers & side dishes   20

Open sandwiches   42

Fish & shellfish   62

Meat, poultry & game   76

Desserts & baking   98

Useful addresses   126

Index and acknowledgements   127

Denmark: a culinary history

Vikings, peasants, aristocrats, seasonal extremes, European alliances, land reforms and the social changes that followed industrialization have all played a role in creating a traditional cuisine that is still valued and enjoyed today.

Dip a spoon into a bowl of sweet beer and rye bread soup or savoury yellow pea soup, or taste dried cod, smoked pork, salt-cured salmon and pickled herring. These simple dishes have been enjoyed since Denmark's medieval period. Dried cod has an even longer history, starting with the Vikings who sailed the high seas in the 10th century, provisioned with protein-rich dried fish as well as nuts, berries, apples, venison, geese, chicken and mutton.

Many historic Danish dishes are still popular and widely enjoyed, even if some are today considered old-fashioned. They're still being served because they taste good, and because affluence came late to this northern European country. Only since World War II has life become quite so sweet as

it is today for Danes, so the connection between past and present is still strong. Add the Danes' pride in and nostalgia for their traditional dishes, which contribute to a strong national identity and it's easy to understand why Denmark's culinary traditions still thrive.

Dishes of nobles and peasants

Life during rural Denmark's medieval era was hard. Even mild summers with good harvests might not provide enough food to last through the long, dark winters. In the world's oldest monarchy, peasants and nobles' lives were defined by the laws of feudalism, with peasants toiling in the fields to grow their lord's crops in thin, sandy soil. This made prudent cooks thrifty and resourceful, a quality evident to this day in Denmark.

To cope with the cold climate and short growing season, the traditional Danish diet – like those of the other Nordic countries – was weighted with carbohydrates and fatty, rich foods, meat and fish, with few greens or fresh fruit. Denmark's isolation at the top of Europe, as well as its geography of numerous separate islands that were difficult to reach, meant that most food had to be seasonal and locally produced.

Beer and rye bread were staples for both upper and lower classes. Meat was a luxury. Without refrigeration, storing food meant salting, pickling or drying it; smoking was reserved for special foods such as eel because wood was available only in limited amounts. (Peat was the prime source of heat in Denmark.) Fruit was eaten in season or dried. The large summer catches of herring were pickled or salted, using imported salt.

Denmark's royal licence inns, or *kroer*, date from the medieval period. In 1283, King Erik Klipping decreed that inns should be established at intervals along roads and at ferry landings to guarantee the monarch lodgings while travelling about the realm. Many of these old country inns have not changed since the 1700s, and are noted for preserving and serving traditional Danish dishes.

Left During the medieval period life was very hard for ordinary Danish people, and remnants of the feudal system lingered here much longer than in the rest of Europe.

International influences

In the 17th and 18th centuries Denmark consolidated its position as a Baltic superpower, and its nobles mingled with European aristocracy. French cooks were employed, and the Danes adopted roux-based cream soups and sauces, blue cheese, *franskbrød* (French bread), elaborate pastries and poached fish. In time, the new trends filtered down to the expanding middle class. Life became a little easier for nobles and peasants alike in 1719, when Danish farmers started growing potatoes – a reliable, nutritious crop that thrived in the Nordic climate. Potatoes quickly became a staple, eaten with every hot meal.

Austrian and German bakers introduced what was to become Denmark's most iconic food: rich, flaky puff pastry, which arrived in the 1860s, when Copenhagen's native bakers went on strike. The replacement bakers from Austria and Germany brought with them the technique for making the pastry, and after the strike Danish bakers made *weinerbrød* (Vienna bread) their own superb confection.

Agricultural reform

In the mid-19th century Danish land ownership laws were reformed, revolutionizing the country's agriculture. The new system reduced the privileges of the landowning class and encouraged single-owner farms. At the same time, inexpensive grain from the US and Canada began to flood into Europe and the government encouraged its sale and use as animal feed. As a result, the

Right By the 19th century Denmark's prosperity was increasing and festivals like Christmas could be more lavishly celebrated with imported foods.

Right The Danish monarchy is one of the oldest in Europe, and for centuries the contrast between the rich nobility and the subsistence-level poor was stark.

Danish pork, dairy and poultry industries blossomed, and butter, bacon, milk, cheese, eggs and many forms of pork made the Danish diet one of the richest in Europe.

Meanwhile, the manure from all those farm animals enriched Danish soil, turning the country into a lush green patchwork of tidy farms and dramatically expanding the choice of vegetables available. Green and red cabbage, pickled beetroot, cucumber salad, and peas and carrots in white sauce all found their place on the table in the 1800s.

Industrialization in the late 19th and early 20th centuries prompted social change and widened the choice of food. It also helps explain the phenomenon of the *smørrebrød* (open sandwich). This unique Danish culinary invention has its roots in the sandwiches eaten in the fields by farm workers. Both *smørrebrød* and the *koldt bord* (cold table) buffet developed from traditional workers' lunches. As people moved from farms to cities to find work in the late 1800s and early 1900s, such lunches served at cafés and restaurants became popular.

Since then, Danish cuisine has stayed relatively unchanged. The Danes may enjoy trying international dishes, but they also stay fiercely loyal to their own. Since the 1980s, there has been a resurgence of appreciation in Denmark for the country's traditional dishes.

The Danish landscape

Lying at the crossroads between continental Europe and Scandinavia, Denmark is a magical land of low-lying islands and a peninsula stretching into the North Sea. Linked to Norway and Sweden by language and history, the country experiences similar extremes of climate, ranging from blissful, cool summers of endless light to wet, windy and dark winters.

Compared to its Scandinavian neighbours and most other European countries, the Kingdom of Denmark is a small nation and a low one, its land smoothed by receding glaciers in the last Ice Age. In area, the country spans only 43,094 sq km/16,639 sq miles. Of Denmark's 406 named islands, fewer than 100 are inhabited; the 3 largest are Sjælland (Zealand), Fyn (Funen) and Bornholm. There are 5.4 million Danes, and the country's capital city is København (Copenhagen) on Zealand. Germany lies to the south, while to the east is Sweden, the Kattegat and Øresund Channels and the Baltic Sea.

Norway and the Skagerrak Channel lie to the north, while the North Sea washes the west coast. No doubt the proximity of water and its role in transportation contributed to making the early Danes such superb seafarers and ship designers, not to mention fishermen.

Sea, sky and landscape

Warmed by the Gulf Stream, Denmark enjoys a mild climate despite its northerly location. The prevailing winds from the west off the North Sea create billowy cumulus clouds. The landscape is flat, but its features vary between marshland, wooded hills, moors, lakes and farmland. Sandy beaches and steep chalk cliffs add another dimension to the terrain.

Barely 150 years ago, Denmark's soil was mostly poor glacier moraine on which farmers scraped out a precarious living and the people's diet was correspondingly limited. But decades of raising livestock and tilling in manure have improved the land's fertility, making agriculture a leading industry. The Danish menu has expanded accordingly to include many pork products and a greater variety of grains and seeds as well as eggs, cheese, cream and butter.

Ever since the first Dane sailed off in a boat, the waters surrounding Denmark's

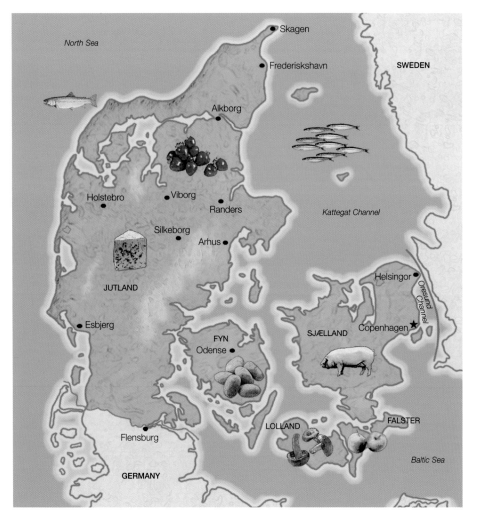

Left Almost surrounded by the sea, Danes have long relied on fish to supplement what they could produce on their farms.

islands and peninsula have been important sources of fish. In summer the herring shoals are harvested along the coast, and in past times, during the fallow winter months, farmers turned fishermen would set out to catch cod, halibut and plaice. Denmark has no major rivers, but fjords reach far inland. These fingers of ocean linking to freshwater streams are where salmon and eels return to spawn in spring.

Denmark's natural vegetation is mixed forest, but just 12 per cent of the country is forested today, due to felling in earlier centuries for building ships and houses. Coniferous trees prevail in the former heath areas of western Jutland, and many dunes along the beaches in north Jutland are forested with spruce and pine. The climate is hospitable to apple orchards, especially on the islands of Lolland and Falster, and plum and cherry trees thrive in gardens.

Magical Copenhagen and Zealand

Zealand has gently rolling hills, long sandy beaches, particularly on the west and north coasts, and prosperous dairy and arable farms in the west and south. Low-lying and accessible from the sea, it's where Germanic tribes first settled 8,000 years ago, followed by Norsemen.

By 1167, when Copenhagen, meaning "merchants' harbour", was officially founded, the city was a significant trading settlement. It still serves as the country's focus for trade, its waterways echoing those of ancient times.

Funen and Bornholm

Denmark's second largest island is Funen. Its west coast is lapped by the Little Belt Channel, and its eastern edge by the Great Belt, both important herring grounds. In the south-west, on a wooded moraine ridge called the Funen Alps, the fertile soil yields an abundance of vegetables including corn, tomatoes and cucumbers, plus flowers and fruit grown in tidy, straight-edged fields and orchards. It is often called the country's granary, and is one of the wealthier regions of Denmark.

Ferries leave nightly from Copenhagen to make the seven-hour voyage to Bornholm, lying south-east of Zealand in the Baltic Sea. For centuries, the island served as a defensive outpost for Copenhagen against Sweden. Today, its fertile, rolling hills are forested or farmed, set with thousand-year-old churches, manor houses and village inns. A temperate climate, with long hours of sunlight, (the most in Denmark) produces

Left and above Agriculture centres around family farms where the country's soil, enriched by years of pig and chicken production, yields golden rye and oats.

lush gardens, fields of mustard, rapeseed and grain, and meadows where figs, cherry, chestnut and mulberry trees flourish.

Jutland connections

The Jutland Peninsula is Denmark's link with the rest of Europe. Unlike picturesque Funen and Zealand, Jutland is more rugged. A region of thriving pig farms and dairies, Jutland is sliced by the craggy Limfjord, a shallow sound that reaches in from the west coast and bisects its northern tip.

Each area of Jutland has its own special nature. East Jutland features a network of lakes and forests around the town of Silkeborg. In summer, its woodlands are lush with wild raspberries, strawberries and blueberries, and later, wild mushrooms. In the north, beautiful sand dunes and white beaches have long been a destination for tourists and artists seeking the radiant Nordic light. On the west coast, the soil favours wild pors (bog myrtle) and juniper berries, used in making aquavit.

Danish cuisine

The Danish cook's talent for making much out of a little reflects the difficulties of living off the land in a cold climate, but this frugality does not extend to entertaining. Danes have a deep-rooted sense of wellbeing, which is expressed in the enjoyment of dining with family and friends.

It's long been said that Danes love to eat, and eat well. But there's a deeper meaning behind this statement. Underlying the Danish attitude to good food is one of the bedrocks of social culture: the concept of *hygge*. There is no literal English translation for *hygge*. It's best described as mental and physical contentment, the security and warmth connected with good feelings about home and family. *Hygge* includes eating and drinking with family and friends in a convivial atmosphere of generous hospitality and comfort. It includes candles, pleated napkins, a beautifully set table and gracious hosts. It's an essential part of the national psyche.

Hygge also explains why almost all entertaining in Denmark takes place at home, which is still the focus of Danish culture. Home is where the host or hostess can spread out a *koldt bord* (cold table) with an abundance of assorted dishes, both cold and hot, several varieties of cheese, breads, schnapps, coffee and cakes to create a warm and welcoming atmosphere. Restaurants are reserved for business socializing or special occasions such as Christmas luncheons, and countryside inns, or *kroer*, are popular for spring or holiday excursions.

Enduring rural tradition

No doubt the concept of *hygge* stems from living in a cold, inhospitable climate. Although no one ever starved to death in Denmark (or so the joke goes), in earlier centuries seasonal extremes made survival challenging. Making a living, and having enough food in your storehouse to last until the next harvest was a source of deep contentment and something worth celebrating, as well as worth being frugal about.

An appreciation of good food was established during Denmark's rural era, when the climate acutely affected the life and livelihood of the average labourer. If you were a peasant facing uncertain meals, you ate whatever and whenever you could, but even so, eating was also about creating an atmosphere of wellbeing, whatever your class. The first Danish cookbook, published in 1616, was a directive to aristocrats about how to achieve an elegant courtly table with nationally produced seasonal fare.

A history of living close to nature gives Danes, and most Scandinavians, a special appreciation for seasonal foods even today. The first spring asparagus and the first strawberries of summer are causes for celebration. Copenhagen's finest restaurants annually vie for the prestige of serving the first new potatoes, particularly from the island of Samsø – regardless of cost – and the event is sure to make the evening news.

From five meals a day to three

Rural life is the source for Denmark's plain dishes and straightforward eating traditions. In agrarian times, work

Left During Denmark's agrarian era, the preserving, pickling, drying and storing of food was essential for surviving the far north's long, harsh winters.

Left First built in the 13th century to guarantee lodging for royalty touring the countryside, royal inns or kro still serve traditional Danish fare.

schedules meant five meals spaced through the day to maintain energy; the midday meal was typically bread and butter eaten in the fields. Hearty, high-carbohydrate and high-fat meals served as insulation against cold winters and draughty lodgings. Today, with rich country dishes still mainstays of the everyday diet, an active lifestyle – the bicycle is the most common form of transport in Denmark – means there are few Danes who qualify as overweight.

Three meals per day became the norm with the arrival of the industrial era. *Morgenmad* (breakfast), with bread and butter, sliced cheese, pickled herring and perhaps an egg, is followed by *frokost* (lunch) between 12 and 2 pm. This meal might be *smørrebrød* or a packed lunch from home. *Aftensmad* (dinner), eaten between 6 and 8 pm, is the hot meal, for which families gather. During the week it is generally one course, but soup, a main course and dessert (a pudding or cheese) may be served at weekends.

Coffee and pastries generally follow a little later in the evening, with a small glass of liqueur if there are guests. But Danes have a knack for adding extra meals. Late morning or afternoon coffee with Danish pastry is a favourite for a work break.

Denmark's beer culture

Drinking beer is a Danish custom that dates back to before Viking times, although in pre-Christian history it would have been mead, a fermented honey beverage. For centuries, beer was served with every meal, including breakfast. The brewing cycle started in March, with a waning moon. There was also a winter brew around 9 December, to be ready by the winter equinox or St Thomas' Eve on 20 December. Food is not a necessary accompaniment to beer for a Dane, but some insist that only with a glass of beer or schnapps is the experience of *smørrebrød* complete.

Scandinavian links

There are many similarities between Danish cuisine and the menus of other Scandinavian countries, particularly Norway, due to their shared climate and political and cultural histories. Denmark ruled Norway for four centuries. Copenhagen and Bergen were both members of the Hanseatic League and the countries exchanged goods and services along with inhabitants.

Cooks in both countries make almond ring cakes, and dried or salted cod is a shared classic dish, as are pickled beets and cucumber salad. The differences are in the nuances: cloudberries and lingonberries are native to Norway, where herring is smoked and potatoes are rarely caramelized as they are in Denmark. Swedes and Danes both adore yellow pea soup, crispbread and cheeses, but the Danes are more apt to eat pork, while Swedes and Norwegians prefer fish and lamb.

Below Ablaze with candles, even bars in Denmark promote a cosy, convivial atmosphere to extend the concept of *hygge*, or wellbeing and contentment.

Danish festivals and holidays

A blend of sacred and secular rituals defines Denmark's key holidays. Many of these annual events have their roots in ancient pagan traditions, while others reflect the country's early Catholic era and subsequent shift to the Lutheran faith.

By law, public holidays fall on the same days as those of the Danish National Church. Other holidays mark historic dates or the seasonal swings from brilliant summer to deep winter darkness. Special foods are part of many celebrations.

New Year's Eve
Exchanging visits with family and friends to enjoy wine and small cakes is the traditional pastime as the year winds to a close. The wine, often a homemade vintage made from garden currants or cherries, is served with small cakes or biscuits such as mazarins, macaroons and vanilla rings. At 6 pm Queen Margrethe II delivers her annual speech on television, and families enjoy a supper of baked or poached cod with potatoes, cauliflower, aquavit and beer.

Fastelavn
Once a period of fasting, *Fastelavn* (Shrovetide) on the Monday before Lent begins has become a carnival-like event for children. They wake their parents by "beating" or tickling them with birch branches called *Fastelavnsris*, wear fancy costumes to school and feast on *Fastelavnsboller*, sweet, cream-filled Lenten buns, which they are given by their neighbours.

Easter
When the first snowdrops appear in the spring garden, *Påske* (Easter) is just around the corner. Danes celebrate by sending anonymous messages called *gækkebreve* (guessing letter), which are poems decorated with papercuts and snowdrops. If the recipient can't guess the name of the sender, they owe them an Easter egg. Easter lasts from Wednesday to the following Monday, prompting lavish lunch parties, specially brewed beer and many glasses of aquavit. On Easter Sunday the main meal can include lamb, chicken or fish. If the first asparagus has appeared, it's a special side dish.

Store Bededag
Celebrated on the fourth Friday after Easter, this exclusively Danish holiday is called Great Prayer Day. In Copenhagen,

Below left Like the rest of Europe, Easter egg hunts and chocolate eggs are a big part of the holiday.

Below right On *Store Bededag*, Danes walk along the boulevard on the waterfront where the Little Mermaid keeps her vigil.

Far left Women in national costume cook *æbleskiver*, the Danish doughnut.

Left On Midsummer Eve huge bonfires burn along the coast, blazing into the sky.

residents traditionally promenade along the city's ramparts in their new spring clothes, then feast on *varme hveder*, square wheat biscuits served warm.

Valborgsaften
Celebrated on 30 April in Jutland, *Valborgsaften* (Walpurgis Eve) is the time when peasant folk believed witches on broomsticks and other demons rode through the night to visit the Devil. Building hilltop bonfires kept the evil spirits from stopping to harm farms and villages – as well as burning up the garden's winter refuse.

Whitsun
"White Sunday", or Pentecost, is marked with songfests by choral societies, plus vigorous cleaning at home. It is considered spring's official beginning when Danes rise early "to see the sun dance" after the long winter, and coffee must be ready on the table in the garden by 6 am. On the following Monday people go on country walks or bicycle rides to look for the first leaves appearing on the beech trees (the beech is Denmark's national tree). They celebrate with picnics or patio parties, and dine at

kroer, where the season's first elver or eel, a speciality of these old inns, may be on the menu.

Constitution Day
On 5 June 1849, King Frederick VII signed Denmark's first constitution. On the same day in 1953, King Frederick IX signed another that declared Denmark a democratic parliamentary monarchy. The date coincides with early rhubarb, which inspired the National Day dessert, often served following cold roast chicken, cucumber salad and potato salad.

Midsummer Eve
Marking St Hansaften (St John's Eve) and the summer solstice, when daylight in the far north never ends, 23 June is celebrated with folk dancing, speeches, singing, bonfires, feasts and all-night parties. An effigy of a witch (a symbol of winter or death) is sometimes burnt in an ancient ritual condemning evil spirits forever to the fires of hell.

Mortensaften
An old family holiday, *Mortensaften* (St Martin's Eve) on 11 November celebrates the harvest and the legend

that St Martin, reluctant to become a bishop, hid in a barn until some geese alerted the searchers to his hiding place. Perhaps as retribution, a fine meal with goose as the main course is served, followed by *æbleskiver* (doughnuts).

Christmas
In the weeks before 24 December, houses are scrubbed, cakes and biscuits are prepared, farm animals are tended with extra care, sheaves of grain are put out to feed birds, the fir tree is cut or purchased, and gifts are gathered and wrapped. Danish brewers produce special Christmas beers, and employers host Christmas lunches for their employees and colleagues.

On *Lille Julaften* (little Christmas Eve), on 23 December, friends and families gather for *glögg* (spiced wine) and *æbleskiver* dusted with icing sugar and served with jam. Christmas candles are lit and every house glows.

On *Julaften* (Christmas Eve), families gather for three days of celebrations. Following afternoon church services, people enjoy a lavish Christmas feast, featuring roast goose, duck or turkey, gravy, red cabbage, boiled potatoes, mashed parsnips or carrots, and always rice pudding for dessert. The *jule-nisse*, the elusive, red-capped, Christmas farm elf, is remembered with his own bowl of rice pudding to ensure good luck in the coming year. After dinner, the family sings carols, dances round the Christmas tree, opens presents and eats marzipan and biscuits with coffee.

The Danish open sandwich

With the open sandwich, the Danes have created something sublime using the simple starting point of a single slice of humble rye bread spread with butter. Assembling an open sandwich is a straightforward adventure with a delicious ending.

Topped with lavish combinations of meat, fish, cheese, pâté or even sliced new potatoes, with eye-catching garnishes that provide accents of flavour and texture, *smørrebrød* (literally "buttered bread") is unquestionably a Danish original. It is eaten with a knife and fork and is traditionally enjoyed as a cold lunch on weekdays or on Saturday evenings with family and friends. The toppings range from rustic pairings to poetic flights of fancy with names like Fairy's Delight, the Rush Hour and Lovers' Tryst; there are combinations named in honour of Hans Christian Andersen, Princess Alexandra and even the British Union Jack.

No one quite knows the origin of *smørrebrød*. Some speculate that it derives from the portable lunches of peasants working in the fields. Others trace its beginnings to the medieval custom of eating off bread "trenchers" instead of plates – the gravy-soaked leftovers would be left for the serfs and village poor to eat. The first mention of *smørrebrød* in Denmark is in the writings of the playwright Ludvig Holberg (1684–1754), who described the diet of the upper class as "soup, salt meat or *smørrebrød*". The tradition no doubt expanded over the decades as housewives discovered its virtues in using up cold leftovers. Despite the incursion of 21st-century fast food, most Danes still pack open sandwiches for their weekday lunch breaks.

Open sandwiches inspired an entire category of restaurants in Copenhagen. In 1888, Oskar Davidsen, a Copenhagen wine merchant, founded a *smørrebrød* restaurant under his name. More than a century later it's still going strong, now owned and managed by Ida Davidsen, Oskar's great-granddaughter. It offers over 300 *smørrebrød* choices, printed on a menu more than 1.2m/4ft long. In 1910, Slotskaelderen hos Gitte Kik was opened in a basement just across from the Christiansborg Palace (where Parliament convenes) and today it still exclusively serves open sandwiches in classic combinations.

When making *smørrebrød* there are few rules beyond buttering the bread with a lavish layer of salted butter, completely hiding the bread with the *pålæg* (topping), selecting harmonizing garnishes and creating a beautiful sandwich with the highest quality ingredients. But be advised: Danes take their *smørrebrød* traditions seriously.

How to create an open sandwich

To get started, prepare all the ingredients and set them out so you can work assembly-line style, selecting what you need to build each sandwich from the buttered bread up. Consider yourself an

Far left In Danish bars and food stores, the wide variety of open sandwiches available is assembled by a specially-trained *smørrebrødsjomfru*, or 'smørrebrød maid'.

Left If you are making an open sandwiches for guests, make two or three kinds. Serve on a wooden board or platter, and always serve fish ones first, then meat.

Left Rye bread is the preferred base for an authentic Danish sandwich, spread with plenty of good Danish butter.

artist working with a palette of ingredients to create delicious, aesthetically pleasing *smørrebrød*. Your goal is to create sandwiches that are a feast for the eye as well as the appetite.

Bread is the beginning

Thin slices (3–5mm/⅛–¼in) of firm, dense-grained rye bread (choose light, dark or wholegrain) or pumpernickel are favoured for meat, fish or cheese. Toppings with delicate flavours such as prawns (shrimp) and mild cheeses are served on crusted white bread, or what Danes call *franskbrød* (French bread).

A serving is generally based on a half-slice of bread, measuring about 5 x 10cm/2 x 4in. If you are planning a *smørrebrød* party, allow three to four sandwiches this size per person. Most can be made a few hours ahead and refrigerated until you're ready to serve.

Butter comes next

On top of the bread comes a luscious thick layer of salted butter. Butter adds flavour to the toppings and acts as a moisture barrier, keeping the bread from becoming soggy, so it should always be spread right to the edges. Choose high-quality Danish butter if it's available.

Traditionally, lard, bacon fat and even duck or goose dripping would be used under roast pork, sausages, liver pâté or new potatoes to enhance their flavours.

Sandwich toppings

Generally a single ingredient stars in an open sandwich, but the number of possible toppings is limited only by the imagination. In fact, it's often said that anything edible can be used to make open sandwiches. Danish favourites include liver pâté, ham, roast pork, game or poultry, baby prawns (shrimp), pickled herring, smoked eel, sliced potatoes, cheeses, sliced eggs, salads and many, many more.

Meats and cheeses can be stacked or rolled to add visual appeal, but on a traditional sandwich the topping should always completely cover or spread beyond the edge of the bread. Lettuce leaves are often used to separate the buttered bread from the topping, the pretty green curled edges further enhancing the arrangement.

Right Frosty glasses of good Danish beer, such as Carlsberg or Tuborg, or thimbles of golden Aalborg aquavit, make the perfect accompaniment to open sandwiches.

Garnishes add an artistic touch

With garnishes, the goal is to create visual appeal with a simple touch, rather than a fussy one. Options include lettuce, watercress, dill and parsley sprigs, curls of cucumber, slices of tomato, egg or radish, a sprinkling of capers, a dollop of good quality remoulade – an accompaniment similar to tartare sauce – that Danes love and serve with almost everything.

Dine like a Dane

To make a meal of open sandwiches, assemble a selection of different types on a large tray or serving platter edged with round (butterhead) lettuce leaves, or place them on a simple wooden cutting board. When it's time to eat, set the table with knives and forks, and pour frosty glasses of beer or schnapps. Always start your meal with herring, fish or prawn sandwiches followed by meat varieties – and enjoy many sips of beer and aquavit in between.

Traditional foodstuffs

Gardens, farms, forests, orchards and the wide ocean have long supplied Danish cooks with a cornucopia of ingredients, and these staple products are still prized as the foundations of traditional home cooking today.

Although Denmark is isolated by geography and climate, its seasonal produce, locally available products and traditional food preservation techniques such as pickling and curing have produced a delicious variety of dishes – a testimony to inventive, careful Danish cooks. The enjoyment of these national products is still alive in Denmark today, and 21st-century cooks still use the traditional ingredients listed here.

Meat, poultry and game

In peasant times, animals were raised on a limited scale, since they required large amounts of feed and Danish soil was not particularly productive. Consequently, the traditional Danish diet included limited amounts of meat and poultry, which were primarily reserved for special occasions and holiday feasts. Wild game, including hares, deer and small fowl, offered some year-round variety.

In the mid-1800s, when cheap North American grain enabled an increase in the farming of pigs, dairy cows and chickens, Danish agriculture reinvented itself with gusto. A greater variety of meat cuts and byproducts became available, and as Danes became more affluent more of their disposable income was available to spend on a richer and more varied diet. Farmed products expanded further in modern times, with veal, lamb and beef finding their place on the weekly menu.

Below Denmark's fishing industry provides the country with a plentiful supply of fresh fish from the seas, fjords and rivers.

Fish and seafood

Surrounded by the sea, the Danes and fishing are inseparable. The connection goes back to pre-history, when fish was sustenance for ancient tribes living on Zealand well before the land was cultivated. Later, farmers headed for the sea during the fallow months of winter to stave off the threat of starvation before the first crops could be harvested. The Skagerrak and Kattegat Channels on the west and east sides of Jutland, the Baltic Sea around Bornholm, the west coast of Norway and the North Atlantic were all prime fishing grounds. Coldwater fish such as herring, plaice, cod, Dover sole, halibut, flounder, salmon and prawns (shrimp), if not eaten fresh, were dried, salted or pickled using age-old preservation methods.

Most of the catch is sold through local wholesalers and auctions. Copenhagen has Denmark's only official fish market, established in the 1940s. As pork products took precedence in the Danish diet, fish lost some of its importance, though consumption is now rising again. Smoked and fresh eel, Greenland prawns, *gravad laks* (salt-cured salmon), cod, lumpfish roe and, of course, pickled herring, are steadfast favourites.

Dairy products

Denmark's farms, both past and present, have yielded some of the world's highest quality dairy products. In the old agrarian-based Denmark, farmers

produced butter, cheese, milk and eggs purely for local consumption, and this well-established system set the stage for the co-operative movement in the 1860s, when individual farmers teamed up to process and market their products more widely.

Used for cooking and flavouring, in savoury dishes as well as desserts and baking, the quality of Danish butter is superb. It was originally made on individual farms – along with cheese – as a way to preserve an abundance of spring and summer milk. Danish butter is churned from cultured rather than sweet cream and has a low water content, making it ideal for pastry-making and all kinds of baking.

The Danes' many regional and national cheeses have long added richness and flavour to their diet. Traditional cheeses range from soft to firm and include: Samsø, a mild, Swiss-style cheese named after the island where it originated; Danbo, firm with a buttery flavour; Esrom, a semi-soft, pungent cheese that grows stronger as it ages; Havarti, semi-firm with a network of tiny holes; Tilsit, a stronger-flavoured version of Havarti; a Danish version of Port Salut;

and mellow-tasting Tybo, made with or without caraway seeds. Influenced by French chefs, Danish cheese makers also produce Camembert and outstanding blue cheeses. Danes enjoy eating cheese on buttered rye bread for breakfast, and often include a cheese board at the end of a meal, but will rarely cook with cheese.

Eggs have always had priority over chickens in Denmark. Following a farmer's logic, why kill the bird if its product provides income? For many years, this philosophy made chicken an expensive food, and it was reserved for special occasions such as Sunday dinner and family parties. Only since the mid-20th century has it become more widely available and affordable.

Garden produce

The Danish garden overflows with vegetables. Poor soil once limited the selection to hardy cruciferous species and the sturdy potato, but the 19th-century shift to pig and poultry production had positive results for home gardens as well as farms. The well-fertilized soil, along with the long summer days and a generally cool climate, create

hospitable growing conditions for cabbages, cucumbers, carrots, radishes, beetroot (beet), white and red onions, leeks, turnips and parsnips. Some vegetables – notably cucumbers, beetroot and red cabbage – are pickled for year-round use, while others, such as cabbages, parsnips, turnips and onions, are preserved in cold storage.

Danish cooks grow and use basic herbs in their cooking, either dried or fresh depending on the season. Parsley, dill, chives, thyme, marjoram and horseradish top the list of herbs used most often in traditional dishes.

Berries and fruits

From the first June strawberries to summer's raspberries, blueberries, currants, elderberries and gooseberries, soft fruits are eagerly anticipated and treasured. Grown in gardens as well as harvested wild, berries are used to make cordials, sauces for meat and poultry, desserts, fruit soups and fillings for Danish pastries or layer cakes.

Lingonberries, which are related to cranberries, are not native to Denmark but grow wild in Norway and Sweden. They're a favourite turned into a sauce to serve with meat and poultry.

Apples, plums and cherries are cultivated in gardens as well as commercial orchards, and are used in a variety of traditional dishes, from apple cake to the cherry sauce served with Christmas rice pudding. Pears also grow fairly well, but produce small fruit due to the cool climate. Rhubarb is another home-grown favourite. Traditional recipes for dried and pickled fruit date from the age before refrigeration.

Potatoes

No Danish hot meal would be complete without potatoes. They were first planted in Denmark in 1642 in the Royal Botanical Garden, but not until 1719 did Danish farmers start cultivating them. Their popularity spread, even inspiring a dish based exclusively on the first small,

Left to right A bowl of gooseberries, redcurrants, blueberries and raspberries. Dried pear and apple rings and prunes. Three types of Danish crispbreads.

new potatoes from the island of Samsø. Denmark's small, round red- or brown-skinned potatoes are creamed, candied, mashed, boiled and made into warm or cold potato salads. A third of the total potato crop is eaten for dinner, half is processed as potato flour, and the remainder is used as seed potatoes.

Mushrooms

In late summer and autumn, the Scandinavian woodlands burst with wild mushrooms. Trained from childhood to identify the best edible varieties – and to know where to find them – people head into the forests to forage for species such as ceps (porcini) and chanterelles and several kinds of truffle. Sliced and simply sautéed in butter and finished with cream, wild mushrooms accompany pork or beef dishes. Many Danish cooks dry mushrooms for winter use.

Bread, crispbread and pastries

As in all of Scandinavia, bread is an essential part of Danish meals, truly the staff of life. Most is made from rye, a grain that tolerates the northern climate. A traditional dark, heavy, sourdough rye bread, *rugbrød*, is sold pre-sliced ready

for *smørrebrød*, and forms the basis for a *rugbrødsmad* (rye bread meal), meaning a regular lunch. Other forms of bread, made with yeast or sourdough, range from light rye to wholegrain. Rye is also used to make a variety of crisp, flat, cracker-style breads, which store well.

White bread, made with wheat flour and yeast, is also a staple on the Danish table, a link to the country's historic connection with France. Called *franskbrød* (French bread), it's often eaten with jam for breakfast, and serves as the base for *smørrebrød* topped with prawns (shrimp) or smoked salmon.

Danes also absolutely love eating pastries, and can easily find reasons to enjoy a late morning or afternoon cup of coffee with a freshly baked treat. Commercial pastry shops thrive, but even in busy, modern times, home baking is popular. From *boller* – small, plump yeast rolls served plain, studded with candied fruits or filled with cream and iced – to *kringler* – filled traditional Danish pastries shaped like pretzels – there are myriad variations. Pastries are an essential part of entertaining in Denmark, served with coffee after dinner or in the afternoon.

Hornsalt

An ancestor of baking soda, *hjortetaksalt* (salt of hartshorn) is ammonium carbonate, a white powder originally ground from the antlers of reindeer. Known as baker's ammonia, it's used primarily by Scandinavian bakers (past and present) to make biscuits lighter and crisper. It has an unpleasant ammoniac odour, but this disappears in cooking.

Marzipan

Finely ground almonds are blended with sugar and sometimes egg whites to make this moderately sweet, pliable dough, which can be moulded into shapes and coloured with food colouring. Pastry chefs roll it into sleek sheets to mould over layer cakes or use as pastry fillings. At Christmas, families often spend an evening making small marzipan fruits and animals to eat during the holidays. A fat marzipan pig is the traditional prize for whoever finds the whole almond in his or her bowl of Christmas rice pudding.

Left to right Homemade marzipan. Caraway seeds, cinnamon, cardamom pods and cloves. A glass of aquavit.

Spices and seasonings

Danish cooks use many spices, a legacy of the nation's trading and seafaring history and French culinary influences. The US Virgin Islands in the Caribbean were once a Danish colony and served as a source for spices as well as brown sugar. White sugar, once an expensive ingredient, was used sparingly, and most traditional Danish desserts are only slightly sweet. The list of favourite spices includes cinnamon, ginger, cloves, cardamom and vanilla, plus caraway seeds for rye bread and cheeses. Dried mustard, white pepper, salt, distilled vinegar and cider vinegar are standard savoury seasonings.

Alcoholic drinks

Danes are serious beer drinkers. It's a tradition that runs deep, beginning in pre-Christian times when beer was linked with harvest festivals and winter equinox rituals. Hops were first used to brew beer in 13th-century Denmark, and the country's first brewery was established in 1454 in Copenhagen. Before then, everyone made beer at home. Science didn't become part of the brewing process until the 19th century.

Emil Christian Hansen, a brewer working for Carlsberg, is credited with the discovery of a special brewer's yeast that revolutionized the beer industry – not just in Denmark, but worldwide.

Every *Julefrokost* (Christmas lunch) in Denmark requires an ice-cold bottle of *akvavit* (aquavit) on the table. Distilled from potatoes or grain in the same fashion as vodka, the fiery drink is subtly flavoured with herbs such as caraway seeds, anise, dill and coriander. Aalborg is the major Danish distiller. It's also a ritual to drink a thimble or three of crystal clear or golden aquavit – the colour is determined by age – chased by beer, when dining on *smørrebrød* (open sandwiches) or feasting at a *koldt bord* (cold table).

Glögg (spiced or mulled wine) is another popular Christmas drink, and in the cold Danish winter it is wonderfully warming. Adopted from Sweden, *glögg* is made by mixing red wine, a generous splash of aquavit, and spices such as cinnamon and cardamom, with raisins and sliced almonds It is simmered in a big pot on the stove, and served in small cups, accompanied by *æbleskiver,* the traditional Danish doughnuts.

Appetizers &
side dishes

Yellow pea soup with
horseradish cream

Cauliflower soup
with prawns

Chicken soup

Liver pâté

Tartlets

Pickled herring

Herring marinated in sherry

Lemon-marinated salmon
with horseradish

Danish caviar with toast
and crème fraîche

Jerusalem artichokes
au gratin

Braised red cabbage

Pickled beetroot

Cucumber salad

Potato salad

Local ingredients and seasonal flavours

The cold northerly climate, the peasant culture of past centuries and traditional preservation methods such as pickling and salting, along with an inherent Scandinavian sense of economy, all play a role in creating Danish menus. Appetizers and side dishes are straightforward and seasonal, hearty and uncomplicated and exhibit the Danish talent for making a little go far.

Herring, either pickled or bathed in a cream or curry sauce, is a required appetizer at almost every meal, even breakfast. Caviar, from the North Atlantic lumpfish, stands in for costly sturgeon roe, and is quite delicious if not so exotic. Soups and sauces, while simple, are often finished with cream, a luxurious benefit of Denmark's successful dairy industry. Vegetable side dishes are generally simmered or boiled even when they're not potatoes. Salt, pickling spices, vinegar, lemon, dill, thyme, chives, cream, horseradish and onions for additional zip are about as complex as Danish seasonings get in these wholesome dishes.

Since most entertaining happens at home, it's not uncommon to be greeted with a table spread with numerous appetizers. Called a *koldt bord* (cold table), this buffet, similar to the Swedish *smörgåsbord*, generally includes several varieties of pickled herring, paper-thin slices of *gravad lax* (salt-cured salmon), liver pâté, pressed meats, wholegrain rye bread and crispbread, a delectable assortment of creamy and tangy cheeses, and much more – in short, everything needed to make your own open sandwiches. To accompany the *koldt bord*, aquavit and Danish beer are the required drinks. Faced with such a feast, the appropriate response is to gaze into the eyes of your companions and toast "*Skål!*"

450g/1lb dried yellow peas, picked over

500g/1¼lb meaty ham bone or boneless pork shoulder

1 onion, chopped

3 carrots, sliced

3 medium leeks, sliced

10g/2 tsp dried thyme

175ml/6fl oz/¾ cup crème fraîche mixed with 15ml/1tbsp creamed horseradish

salt and ground white pepper

75ml/5 tbsp chopped fresh parsley, to garnish

Cook's tip If whole yellow peas are not available, this soup is equally delicious made with split yellow peas, or green peas, either whole or split.

Yellow pea soup with horseradish cream
Gule ærte med peberrod crème fraîche

Yellow pea soup is a wintertime favourite served throughout Scandinavia, with every country claiming ownership. A traditional country dish full of rib-sticking goodness, there are many variations depending on what vegetables are included (and what's in the pantry) and whether the soup is made with a ham bone or pork shoulder. Split peas speed up the process, but traditional Danish cooks favour whole peas.

1 Put the dried peas in a large, heavy pan and add cold water to cover. Leave to soak overnight.

2 Rinse the peas under cold running water. Return the peas to the pan and add 1.75 litres/3 pints/7½ cups water and the ham bone. Bring to the boil, skim off any foam, lower the heat, cover and simmer for 1 hour until the peas are almost tender.

3 Add the onion, carrots, leeks and thyme, and season to taste with salt and pepper. Cook for about 1 hour more, until the vegetables are tender. Remove the ham bone, slice off any meat and return it to the soup. Correct the seasoning and serve sprinkled with parsley and a dollop of horseradish cream.

Per portion Energy 248kcal/1051kJ; Protein 21.6g; Carbohydrate 32.8g, of which sugars 5.3g; Fat 4.3g, of which saturates 1.2g; Cholesterol 9mg; Calcium 69mg; Fibre 7.4g; Sodium 348mg.

Cauliflower soup with prawns
Blomkålsuppe med rejer

Considered the most elegant member of the cabbage family, cauliflower is much appreciated in Denmark. Along with its rustic cabbage cousins, it is a favourite in Danish kitchen gardens. In this simple old-fashioned recipe, cauliflower is elevated into an elegant, creamy soup prettily garnished with sweet, pink prawns.

1 Put the cauliflower into a large pan and add 1.5 litres/2½ pints/6¼ cups water and the salt. Bring to the boil and cook over a medium heat for 12–15 minutes until tender. Remove 475ml/16fl oz/2 cups of the cooking liquid and reserve. Cover the pan and keep warm.

2 Melt the butter in a separate pan over a medium heat, and stir in the flour to make a smooth paste. Cook, stirring constantly, for 3–5 minutes until the roux is pale beige. Slowly stir in the cream. Remove from the heat and stir in the egg yolk.

3 Stir the reserved cauliflower water into the roux and cook over a low heat, stirring constantly, until the mixture thickens. Do not allow it to boil or it will curdle. Add the cream mixture to the cauliflower. Season with salt and pepper. Divide the soup among six warm soup plates and garnish with a few prawns. Serve immediately.

Per portion Energy 294kcal/1217kJ; Protein 13.3g; Carbohydrate 9.7g, of which sugars 4.6g; Fat 22.6g, of which saturates 13.3g; Cholesterol 159mg; Calcium 95mg; Fibre 2.6g; Sodium 121mg.

Serves 6

1 large cauliflower (about 800g/ 1¾lb trimmed and chopped)

5ml/1 tsp salt, or to taste

25g/1oz/2 tbsp butter

35g/1¼oz/¼ cup plain (all-purpose) flour

250ml/8fl oz/1 cup whipping cream

1 egg yolk, beaten

salt and ground white pepper

225g/8oz cooked small prawns (shrimp), to garnish

Cook's tips
• Season the cream mixture with 5ml/1 tsp curry powder.
• Purée the cauliflower before adding the cream mixture for a smooth soup.

Serves 8–10

1 chicken, about 2kg/4½lb

350g/12oz beef bone

2 bay leaves

3 large leeks, sliced

1 parsnip, thinly sliced

4 carrots, thinly sliced

6 celery sticks, sliced

salt

75ml/5 tbsp chopped fresh parsley, to garnish

For the dumplings

350g/12oz/3 cups plain (all-purpose) flour

125g/4oz/½ cup butter

4 eggs

5ml/1 tsp sugar

salt

Cook's tips The dumplings can be made in advance, and warmed up in the soup just before serving. To make the dumplings a consistent size, spoon the dough into an icing bag without a nozzle. Squeeze out the dough in small amounts, cutting off 5mm/¼ in pieces using kitchen scissors.

Chicken soup
Hønsekodssuppe

A favourite appetizer for a special gathering such as a christening, wedding, anniversary party or confirmation – all highlights on the Danish social calendar – versatile chicken soup is an essential part of every Danish cook's repertoire. In this version, a rich chicken stock is prepared using a whole chicken. The chicken can be removed and served separately, and the soup eaten with the dumplings. Or the chicken can be pulled from the bones, shredded and added to the soup.

1 Bring 3 litres/5 pints/12½ cups water to the boil in a large pan. Add the chicken, beef bone and bay leaves to the pot, and return to the boil. Skim, lower the heat and simmer for 1 hour.

2 Add the leeks, parsnip, carrots and celery to the chicken stock and season with salt. Simmer for about 20 minutes, until the vegetables are tender.

3 Meanwhile, make the dumplings. Place the flour in a mixing bowl. Bring 250ml/8fl oz/1 cup water to the boil in a small pan, add the butter and return to the boil. Stir the mixture into the flour, beating vigorously with a fork to blend it smoothly. The dough should pull away from the sides of the bowl. Leave to cool.

4 Beat in the eggs, one at a time, to make a soft dough. Stir in the sugar and salt to taste. Leave the dough to rest for 20 minutes to thicken slightly.

5 Fill a large pan with lightly salted water and bring to the boil. Use a teaspoon to form small (5mm/¼ in), unevenly shaped balls of dough, and drop them one at a time into the simmering water. They will sink to the bottom, then rise to the top when cooked, in 3–5 minutes. Lift out the dumplings with a slotted spoon and set aside until needed.

6 Remove and discard the beef bone from the soup. Lift out the chicken and carve in slices to serve separately, or pull the meat from the bones and return to the soup. Add the dumplings to the soup to warm through, and serve.

Per portion Energy 266kcal/1115kJ; Protein 25.7g; Carbohydrate 24g, of which sugars 6.6g; Fat 7.5g, of which saturates 1.2g; Cholesterol 109mg; Calcium 48mg; Fibre 2.7g; Sodium 86mg.

Liver pâté

Leverpostej

Liver pâté is an absolute must on every formal buffet table in Denmark. In fact, it's practically essential at the breakfast and lunch table in every Danish home seven days a week. While acceptable versions are available in the supermarket, nothing beats the rich, complex flavour of homemade liver pâté. It is traditionally made with pig's liver, but you can substitute the same quantity of chicken livers if they are easier to find.

1 Line one large (1.5 litre/2½ pint/6¼ cup) loaf tin (pan) or terrine, or two smaller loaf tins, with bacon. Lay the rashers across the tin, letting them drape over the edges, and reserving five rashers for later use.

2 Heat the oil in a small frying pan over a medium heat, and cook the onion, stirring, for 4–5 minutes until it becomes transparent. Leave to cool.

3 Preheat the oven to 180°C/350°F/Gas 4. Working in batches if necessary, put three of the reserved bacon rashers with all the remaining ingredients into a blender or food processor and pulse on low speed to blend thoroughly into a smooth, thick mixture.

4 Pour the liver mixture into the prepared loaf tin. Place the remaining two bacon rashers over the top of the pâté. Stand the loaf tin in the centre of a large, deep baking tin (pan) and pour in enough hot water to reach halfway up the sides of the loaf tin. Bake for 1½ to 2 hours. Leave to cool, then chill the pâté in the tin for at least 2 hours before turning out. Run a knife around the edges first to loosen the pâté. Serve in slices on an open sandwich, or with wholegrain bread and pickled gherkins or Pickled beetroots (beets).

Serves 10–12

225g/8oz unsmoked streaky (fatty) bacon rashers (strips)

30ml/2 tbsp vegetable oil

1 medium onion, finely chopped

675g/1½lb pork livers, trimmed

225g/8oz minced (ground) pork

50g/2oz anchovy fillets

15ml/1 tbsp butter

250ml/8fl oz/1 cup whipping cream

3 eggs

2.5ml/½ tsp ground nutmeg

1.5ml/¼ tsp ground allspice

1.5ml/¼ tsp ground cloves

1.5ml/¼ tsp dried thyme

2.5ml/½ tsp dried marjoram

75ml/2½fl oz/⅓ cup sweet Madeira

salt and ground black pepper

Cook's Tip Any extra pâté mixture that doesn't fit in the loaf tin can be successfully baked in ovenproof ramekins. Uncooked pâté can also be frozen for up to one month.

Per portion Energy 366kcal/1514kJ; Protein 13.3g; Carbohydrate 1.2g, of which sugars 1g; Fat 34.3g, of which saturates 14.9g; Cholesterol 214mg; Calcium 33mg; Fibre 0.1g; Sodium 126mg.

Makes 18

200g/7oz/generous 1½ cups plain (all purpose) flour

125g/4½ oz/9 tbsp butter, softened

150ml/¼ pint/⅔ cup cold water, or enough to bind

For the prawn (shrimp) filling:

45g/1½oz/scant ¼ cup butter

20g/¾oz/scant ¼ cup plain (all-purpose) flour

475ml/16fl oz/2 cups single (light) cream

275g/10oz cooked prawns (shrimp)

salt and ground white pepper

25ml/1½ tbsp chopped fresh dill sprigs

For the chicken and asparagus filling:

65g/2½oz/5 tbsp butter

225g/8oz fresh asparagus, cut into 2cm/¾in pieces

15ml/1 tbsp cooking oil

225g/8oz skinless, boneless chicken breasts, cut into 2cm/¾in cubes

20g/¾oz/scant ¼ cup plain (all-purpose) flour

475ml/16fl oz/2 cups single (light) cream

salt and ground white pepper

45ml/3 tbsp chopped fresh parsley, to garnish

Tartlets
Tarteletter

Danes love their yeast-based pastry, wienerbrød, and in Denmark little pre-baked tartlet cases are widely available to be filled with various tasty fillings at home. Use these fillings with the prepared tartlet shells if you can find them, or make the delicious buttery shortcrust pastry below.

1 Preheat the oven to 200°C/400°F/Gas 6. Sift the flour into a large bowl. Cut the butter into small pieces, add to the flour and rub in until the mixture resembles fine breadcrumbs. Gradually add the water and mix to form a dough. On a lightly floured surface, roll out the pastry and cut circles to fit 7cm/2¾in diameter fluted tart tins. Cut a 13cm/5in square of foil to line each pastry shell and fill with a handful of dried peas or beans to help the pastry keep its shape. Chill for at least 30 minutes to rest the pastry, then bake for 10–15 minutes until crisp and golden. Remove the beans and foil for the final 5 minutes.

2 To make the creamed prawn filling, melt the butter in a pan over a medium heat, and stir in the flour. Cook the roux for 3–5 minutes until pale beige. Slowly stir in the cream and cook, stirring constantly, for about 5 minutes, until thickened. Stir the prawns into the sauce and heat gently for 3–4 minutes. Season well.

3 To make the chicken and asparagus filling, melt 25g/1oz/2 tbsp of the butter in a frying pan over a medium heat. Add the asparagus, toss to coat evenly with butter and cook, stirring, for about 4 minutes, until tender. Remove and set aside on a plate. In the same pan, heat the cooking oil over a medium heat. Add the chicken and cook for about 5 minutes, stirring, until it is no longer pink. Set aside.

4 Melt the remaining butter in a pan over a medium heat and stir in the flour. Cook the roux for 3–5 minutes until pale beige-coloured. Slowly stir in the cream and cook, stirring constantly, for about 5 minutes until the sauce has thickened. Add the asparagus and chicken and heat for 3–4 minutes. Season well.

5 Fill half the tart cases with the creamed prawns, and sprinkle with fresh dill. Fill the rest with the chicken and asparagus, and sprinkle with fresh parsley. Serve.

Per portion Energy 274kcal/1138kJ; Protein 9g; Carbohydrate 11g, of which sugars 1.7g; Fat 21.9g, of which saturates 13.4g; Cholesterol 95mg; Calcium 83mg; Fibre 0.6g; Sodium 131mg.

Serves 4

400g/14oz salted herring fillets

250ml/8fl oz/1 cup wine vinegar

250ml/8fl oz/1 cup water

115g/4oz/½ cup sugar

1 carrot, thinly sliced

2 bay leaves

6cm/2½in fresh root ginger, peeled and finely chopped

4cm/1½in fresh horseradish, peeled and finely chopped

10ml/2 tsp mustard seeds

6 allspice berries

1.5ml/¼ tsp ground coriander

1 red onion, thinly sliced

Pickled herring
Spegesild

Despite the Danish fondness for meat, no koldt bord *or "cold table" – Denmark's version of the Swedish* smörgåsbord *– would be complete without several kinds of marinated herring. According to Scandinavian etiquette, dinners always begin with herring and other fish dishes, before changing plates for the buffet's various meat dishes, salads and cheeses. Flat breads or crispbread and wholegrain rye breads make fine partners for any form of pickled herring, with a garnish of sliced onions and an ice-cold glass of beer.*

1 To make the spiced pickled herring, rinse the fillets several times in cold water. Place in a bowl of cold water, cover and refrigerate overnight.

2 Combine the vinegar, water and sugar in a pan; bring to the boil over a medium heat. Watch carefully, and boil, uncovered, for 10 minutes. Add the carrot, bay leaves, ginger, horseradish, mustard seeds, allspice and coriander; cook for another 10 minutes over a medium heat. Remove from the heat and cool.

3 Taste the herring for saltiness. If it is still too salty, rinse the fillets again. Otherwise, drain, cut into 2.5/1in pieces and place in a non-metallic bowl, layering them with onions. Pour the vinegar mixture over the herring and onions. Cover and refrigerate overnight or for up to four days before serving.

Per portion Energy 231kcal/963kJ; Protein 12.5g; Carbohydrate 7.5g, of which sugars 7.5g; Fat 16.6g, of which saturates 1.2g; Cholesterol 32mg; Calcium 10mg; Fibre 0g; Sodium 623mg.

Herring marinated in sherry
Matjes sild

Once considered the food of the poor, salted herring is now popular throughout Scandinavia, to the point where everyone has their own special preparation. Matjes herring are especially coveted for homemade marinades. These plump, young fish are caught in summer in the cold waters of the North Atlantic and are tender and flavoursome. They are gutted, skinned, lightly dry-salted to preserve them and stored in barrels. In this recipe, the addition of tawny sherry or Madeira gives the herring a lovely mellow, sweet taste.

1 Rinse the herring several times in cold water. Place in a bowl of cold water, cover and refrigerate overnight.

2 Taste the herring for saltiness. If it is still too salty, rinse the fillets again. Otherwise, drain and cut into 2.5cm/1in pieces. Place in a non-metallic bowl and scatter the onion slices over the fish.

3 Combine the vinegar, water, sugar, allspice, cloves, bay leaf and sherry or Madeira in a bowl and pour the mixture over the herring and onions. Cover and refrigerate overnight or for up to four days before serving.

Per portion Energy 228kcal/960kJ; Protein 12.8g; Carbohydrate 20.7g, of which sugars 20.4g; Fat 8.4g, of which saturates 0g; Cholesterol 32mg; Calcium 21mg; Fibre 0.2g; Sodium 626mg.

Serves 8–10

400g/14oz (about 4 or 5) salted herring fillets

1 onion, thinly sliced

150ml/¼ pint/⅔ cup distilled white vinegar

150ml/¼ pint/⅔ cup water

25g/1oz/2 tbsp white sugar

12 allspice berries

12 whole cloves

1 bay leaf

250ml/8fl oz/1 cup medium-sweet sherry or Madeira

Serves 8–10

1kg/2¼lb fresh salmon fillet, skin on

75g/3oz/⅓ cup coarse salt

25g/1oz/2 tbsp sugar

10ml/2 tsp ground white pepper

30ml/2 tbsp fresh lemon juice

105ml/7 tbsp chopped fresh dill

½ lemon, thinly sliced, plus extra to garnish

For the dressing

250ml/8fl oz/1 cup sour cream

30ml/2 tbsp double (heavy) cream

45ml/3 tbsp prepared creamed horseradish sauce, or to taste

45ml/3 tbsp chopped fresh dill

salt and ground white pepper

fresh dill sprigs, to garnish

Cook's tip For a cucumber and crème fraîche sauce, mix 250ml/8fl oz/1 cup crème fraîche with 75/3oz/¾ cup peeled, chopped cucumber, 75ml/2½fl oz/⅓ cup sour cream, 30ml/2 tbsp chopped dill, 15ml/1 tbsp lemon juice, with salt and pepper to taste.

Lemon-marinated salmon with horseradish
Citron marineret laks med peberrods sovs

For a celebratory meal there's no finer fish than salmon. Curing it yourself in a blanket of salt and sugar – the preparation known as gravad lax *– is simple and authentically Scandinavian, and you'll revel in the applause when you serve the tender, rosy fillet in paper-thin slices as a sophisticated appetizer. If possible, choose fresh wild Pacific salmon in preference to farmed salmon, and freeze the salmon fillet for up to four hours before preparing it. Serve with a zesty sour-cream horseradish sauce.*

1 Line a baking tin (pan) with a large piece of foil or clear film (plastic wrap), leaving the ends overlapping the sides of the dish. Remove any small pin bones from the salmon with tweezers. Cut small nicks in the skin to allow the salt and seasonings to penetrate, then cut the fillet in half.

2 Stir together the salt, sugar and pepper in a small bowl.

3 Place one piece of salmon skin side down in the lined dish. Drizzle with lemon juice, rub evenly with half the salt mixture and sprinkle with half the dill. Arrange the lemon slices over the fish. Place the second fillet on a board and rub the flesh evenly with the remaining salt mixture, then sprinkle with the remaining dill. Carefully lift the second fillet and place it over the fillet in the dish, turning it skin side up to make a "sandwich".

4 Wrap tightly in the foil or film and weight with a heavy pot or board. Refrigerate for 48 hours, turning the fish twice daily. The salmon will be cured when it turns a deep, bright red and the edges are slightly white from the salt. To serve, cut the salmon into very thin slices and arrange on a serving plate; discard the skin.

5 To make the dressing, stir together the sour cream, double cream, horseradish, dill, salt and pepper, and chill until ready to serve with the salmon. Garnish both the horseradish cream and the salmon with dill sprigs.

Per portion Energy 479kcal/1981kJ; Protein 26.2g; Carbohydrate 0.4g, of which sugars 0.3g; Fat 40.4g, of which saturates 6.4g; Cholesterol 113mg; Calcium 35mg; Fibre 0g; Sodium 169mg.

6 slices good white bread, crusts removed

100g/3¾oz lumpfish caviar

100ml/3½fl oz/scant ½ cup crème fraîche

½ red onion, thinly sliced

60ml/4 tbsp chopped fresh dill

Cook's tip Substitute red lumpfish caviar for the black variety, sour cream for the crème fraîche, and chopped fresh basil leaves for the dill.

Danish caviar with toast and crème fraîche
Stenbiderrogn på riset brød med crème fraîche

Trust the thrifty Danes to devise inexpensive "caviar" from the plentiful lumpfish swimming in North Atlantic waters. The lightly salted black roe is a tasty substitute for the real thing. You don't have to be rich to enjoy the mix of flavours and textures in this simple, classic presentation served with toast wedges, sour cream, thinly sliced red onions and fresh dill.

1 Lightly toast the bread and cut each slice into four triangles. Arrange on a serving plate. Spoon the lumpfish caviar, crème fraîche and dill into separate small bowls, and place on the serving plate. Arrange the red onion on one corner of the plate.

2 Alternatively, spread each toast triangle with lumpfish caviar. Top with a teaspoon of crème fraîche and a slice of red onion, and sprinkle with dill.

Per portion Energy 208kcal/869kJ; Protein 6.5g; Carbohydrate 19.5g, of which sugars 1.8g; Fat 12.1g, of which saturates 7g; Cholesterol 99mg; Calcium 60mg; Fibre 0.6g; Sodium 731mg.

Jerusalem artichokes au gratin
Jordskokkegratin

The Danes have adopted these somewhat overlooked vegetables. Jerusalem artichokes are not related to globe artichokes at all, but to the sunflower, which is why they're sometimes sold as "sunchokes". They have a delightful, nutty flavour and appealing crunch, but choose tubers that are firm and fresh looking, without wrinkles. Peel them before cooking if you wish, or just wash them well. This dish is a lovely accompaniment to roast meat or fried fish.

1 Preheat the oven to 190°C/375°F/Gas 5. Lightly grease an ovenproof dish. Stir together the sour cream and single cream in a mixing bowl and season with salt.

2 Add the Jerusalem artichokes to the cream and toss to coat evenly with the mixture. Spread the artichokes over the bottom of the prepared dish.

3 Sprinkle evenly with the cheese, then the breadcrumbs. Bake for about 30 minutes, until the cheese melts and the top is brown and bubbling.

Per portion Energy 296kcal/1230kJ; Protein 6.9g; Carbohydrate 27.6g, of which sugars 15.5g; Fat 18.1g, of which saturates 11.1g; Cholesterol 52mg; Calcium 186mg; Fibre 4.4g; Sodium 240mg.

Serves 4

250ml/8fl oz/1 cup sour cream

50ml/2fl oz/¼ cup single (light) cream

675g/1½ lb Jerusalem artichokes, coarsely chopped

40g/1½ oz/½ cup grated Danbo cheese

60ml/4 tbsp fresh breadcrumbs

salt

Cook's tip If you can't find Danbo, a mellow yet flavoursome semi-hard cheese, look for Elbo, Havarti, or use a good English Cheddar.

Braised red cabbage
Rød kål

Sweet, tangy red cabbage is a wintertime favourite everywhere in Scandinavia, but nowhere more so than in Denmark. Outstanding paired with roast pork – another Danish favourite – it's also the traditional accompaniment for the Christmas goose or duck. If the blend of sweet, sour and fruity flavours weren't enticing enough, the vivid violet colour would captivate anyone. This vegetable dish looks as good as it tastes.

1 Remove the outer leaves and core of the cabbage and cut into quarters. Thinly chop or shred the cabbage, and place in a large pan. Add 120ml/4fl oz/½ cup water and the vinegar and bring to the boil. Reduce the heat, cover and simmer for 1 hour, stirring occasionally to prevent scorching.

2 Meanwhile, melt the butter in a large frying pan over a medium heat. Stir in the onion and apple and cook for 5–7 minutes until soft.

3 Stir the apples and onions into the cabbage with the sugar, blackcurrant juice or jam, allspice and cloves, and season with salt. Simmer gently for a further 1½ hours. Adjust the seasoning to taste before serving.

Per portion Energy 90kcal/381kJ; Protein 3.1g; Carbohydrate 19.4g, of which sugars 18g; Fat 0.5g, of which saturates 0g; Cholesterol 0mg; Calcium 98mg; Fibre 5g; Sodium 14mg.

Serves 6

1.3kg/3lb red cabbage

50ml/2fl oz/¼ cup distilled white vinegar

25g/1oz/2 tbsp butter

1 medium onion, finely chopped

2 tart apples, peeled, cored and thinly sliced

50g/2oz/¼ cup sugar

120ml/4fl oz/½ cup blackcurrant juice or jam

1.5ml/¼ tsp ground allspice

6 whole cloves

salt

Cook's tip If blackcurrant juice or jam are not available, substitute apple juice or redcurrant jelly.

Serves 6

1.2kg/2½lb fresh beetroot (beets), preferably with stems attached

45ml/3 tbsp distilled white vinegar

For the marinade

120ml/4fl oz/½ cup water

60ml/4 tbsp distilled white vinegar

90g/3½oz/½ cup sugar

1 bay leaf

2.5ml/½ tsp caraway seeds

3 whole cloves

salt and ground black pepper

Cook's tip Leaving the stems and peel on the beetroot until after they are cooked helps to stop the red colour draining out.

Pickled beetroot
Syltede rødbeder

Dark purple beetroot are beloved in Denmark and the rest of Scandinavia, since they thrive even in short northern summers and are highly nutritious. To extend their versatility in the kitchen, they are pickled for use in everything from salads to soups, to serve as side dishes and to garnish open sandwiches.

1 Trim the beetroot stems to 2.5cm/1in, but do not peel the skins or cut the roots. Place 2 litres/3½ pints water and the vinegar in a deep pan and bring to the boil. Add the beetroot, adding more water if necessary to cover them, and simmer for about 45 minutes until tender. Remove from the heat, drain the beetroot, reserving 250ml/8fl oz/1 cup of the cooking liquid, and allow them to cool.

2 To prepare the marinade, combine all the ingredients in a pan and bring to the boil. Remove from the heat, pour into a large bowl and leave until cool.

3 Peel the cooled beetroot and cut them into 5mm/¼in slices. Add the slices to the bowl with the marinade and toss gently to coat. Cover the bowl and refrigerate for 8 hours or overnight.

Per portion Energy 115kcal/490kJ; Protein 2.7g; Carbohydrate 27.4g, of which sugars 26.5g; Fat 0.2g, of which saturates 0g; Cholesterol 0mg; Calcium 39mg; Fibre 2.9g; Sodium 430mg.

Serves 6

1 large English cucumber, about 35cm/14in long

75ml/5 tbsp distilled white vinegar

25g/1oz/2 tbsp white sugar

45ml/3 tbsp chopped fresh dill

salt and ground white pepper

Cook's tip This cucumber salad is served with all kinds of poached fish, especially salmon. The vinegar and sugar can also be mixed into 250ml/ 8fl oz/1 cup sour cream for a richer, cream-style dressing that goes well with fish cakes and fried fish.

Cucumber salad
Agurkesalat

Hothouse cucumbers grow luxuriantly under artificial light and help to dispel the darkness of long Scandinavian winters. As a result, the cucumber is a favourite food in Denmark. The dressing should be perfectly balanced between sweet and sour, with accents of fresh dill. It is important to make this salad shortly before you intend to serve it, so the cucumber retains its crispness and doesn't become soggy.

1 Cut the cucumber into 3mm/⅛in slices and place in a serving bowl.

2 Combine the vinegar, sugar and dill in a small bowl and season with salt and pepper. Pour the dressing over the cucumber slices and toss to coat evenly. Chill until ready to serve.

Per portion Energy 30kcal/125kJ; Protein 0.7g; Carbohydrate 1.1g, of which sugars 1g; Fat 2.6g, of which saturates 1.6g; Cholesterol 8mg; Calcium 26mg; Fibre 0.4g; Sodium 8mg.

Potato salad
Kartoffelsalat

While the potato is now a staple on Danish tables, it wasn't always that way. Though it reached Europe in 1570, the hardy tuber didn't arrive in Denmark until almost two centuries later. Even then there was great resistance to eating it and it took parish priests to lead the way, demonstrating the potato's virtue as a wholesome food. Today, a meal in Denmark would be incomplete without some form of potatoes, and cold potato salad is a year-round favourite.

1 Boil the potatoes in lightly salted water for 20–25 minutes, until tender, then drain and allow to cool. Peel and coarsely chop the potatoes and place them in a large mixing bowl. Add the onion and celery.

2 Meanwhile make the dressing: in a separate bowl, stir together the sour cream, mayonnaise, mustard, celery seed, dill, salt and pepper.

3 Add the dressing to the potatoes and toss gently to coat evenly with the dressing. Adjust the seasoning, cover the bowl and chill until ready to serve.

Per portion Energy 440kcal/1834kJ; Protein 5.2g; Carbohydrate 38.5g, of which sugars 4.9g; Fat 30.5g, of which saturates 7.7g; Cholesterol 42mg; Calcium 50mg; Fibre 2.4g; Sodium 183mg.

Serves 6–8

1.8kg/4lb potatoes

45ml/3 tbsp finely chopped onion

2 celery stalks, finely chopped

250ml/8fl oz/1 cup sour cream

250ml/8fl oz/1 cup mayonnaise

5ml/1 tsp mustard powder

4ml/¾ tsp celery seed

75ml/5 tbsp chopped fresh dill

salt and ground white pepper

Cook's tip Add chopped cucumber, crumbled bacon rashers, or chopped hard-boiled eggs to the potato salad.

Open sandwiches

Pickled herring

Herring in tomato sauce with egg and dill

Marinated herring in sour cream

Potatoes with leeks and herring

Smoked salmon with dill and lemon

Smoked salmon with scrambled eggs

Fried plaice fillet with remoulade

Shooting star

Prawns with egg and cucumber

Ham with Italian salad

Liver pâté with bacon and mushrooms

The veterinarian's evening sandwich

Pork fillet with crispy onion rings

Bacon with apples

Beef tartare with egg yolk, onion and beetroot

Roast beef, remoulade, crispy onions and horseradish

Bread and butter
elevated to an art form

Nowhere is the Danish knack for making much out of a little
demonstrated so thoroughly as with *smørrebrød*, or open
sandwiches. Although not a traditional sandwich, since the
Danes make these original creations using one slice of bread,
and they are always properly eaten with a knife and fork rather
than out of the hand, *smørrebrød* are far more sophisticated
than the simple 'buttered bread' implied by their Danish name.
With assorted layered toppings, called *pålæg* and decorative
greenery, along with vegetable, fruit or lemon slices for
garnishes, open sandwiches are designed to be stunning in
appearance and flavour even when the ingredients are
humble and may combine leftovers from the previous
evening's supper. In fact, artistically arranging ingredients and
colours to please the eye as well as the palate is a
requirement for every open sandwich. No wonder *smørrebrød*
have been celebrated for over three centuries as one of
Denmark's most popular culinary icons. Traditionally, there is
an established way of arranging open sandwiches, which is
strictly followed by the restaurants and specialist shops
preparing and serving them. In this chapter some recipes
follow the prescribed arrangement, but others don't. You can
choose whether to follow tradition or not.

Pickled herring
Spegesild

One custom faithfully followed at Danish smørrebrød parties is always to start the meal with fish or seafood sandwiches. Pickled herring is generally the first choice. No doubt it was also one of the first toppings, since the tangy flavour of the fish is so well enhanced by the piquant taste of robust rye bread.

1 Butter the slices of bread right up to the edges, top with the lettuce leaves and cut each slice in half.

2 Leaving one curl of lettuce visible on each sandwich, arrange five or six pieces of herring evenly over each sandwich.

3 Arrange three onion rings over the herring on each sandwich. Garnish by tucking a parsley sprig under the top piece of herring.

Per portion Energy 186kcal/776kJ; Protein 9.7g; Carbohydrate 12.2g, of which sugars 6.3g; Fat 11g, of which saturates 3.3g; Cholesterol 34mg; Calcium 25mg; Fibre 0.9g; Sodium 526mg.

Makes 4

25g/1oz/2 tbsp salted butter, softened

2 slices rye bread

2 round (butterhead) lettuce leaves

20–24 pieces pickled herring about 2.5cm/1in square

12 small, thinly sliced white onion rings

4 parsley sprigs

Cook's tips

• Use ready-bought pickled herring for this sandwich, or make your own. If the pickled herring is packed with onion rings, use these to garnish the sandwiches.

• Dark, wholegrain rye bread or seeded multigrain bread are also excellent with pickled herring.

Herring in tomato sauce with egg and dill
Tomatsild med æg og dild

Salted herring is remarkably accepting of a variety of flavourings – sweet, spicy or a blend of the two. The fish is salted in autumn to preserve the catch, but the fillets can also be cured later in a bath of vinegar and sugar, with other flavourings. For this sandwich, prepared herring in tomato sauce is topped with egg slices and garnished with red onion rings and dill in a classic combination dear to Danish hearts.

1 To make the tomato herring, place the pickled herring pieces in a mixing bowl. Stir in the onion, red wine vinegar, tomato purée, sherry, salt and white pepper. Adjust seasonings to taste.

2 To make the sandwiches, butter the slices of bread to the edges and cut each slice in half. Arrange the herring pieces on the bread.

3 Garnish each sandwich by arranging three egg slices over the herring, then top with two or three onion rings and tuck a dill sprig into the onions.

Per portion Energy 177kcal/737kJ; Protein 8.9g; Carbohydrate 11.2g, of which sugars 5g; Fat 11g, of which saturates 4.1g; Cholesterol 119mg; Calcium 38mg; Fibre 1.1g; Sodium 363mg.

Makes 4

150ml/¼ pint/½ cup sour cream

2.5ml/½ tsp creamed horseradish

15ml/1 tbsp Pickled Beetroot (beet) juice

3 matjes herring, about 150g/5oz, cut into 2.5cm/1in squares

115g/4oz/½ cup Pickled Beetroot (beets), diced

250g/9oz/1 cup Cucumber Salad, drained and chopped

25g/1oz/2 tbsp salted butter, softened

2 slices rye bread

2 round (butterhead) lettuce leaves

2 hard-boiled eggs, sliced

4 parsley sprigs

salt and ground black pepper

Marinated herring in sour cream
Matjes sild med fløde crème fraîche

Fishermen have plied the seas around Denmark for centuries. Cod, plaice, mackerel and, of course, herring were plentiful in the cold waters of the Baltic Sea, North Sea and the Kattegat Straits between Jutland and Sweden. Silvery herring became a staple in the Danish diet, and the fat, young, reddish-coloured fish called matjes were especially prized for their flavour.

1 Combine the sour cream, horseradish and beetroot juice in a mixing bowl. Stir in the herring, beetroot and cucumber salad; toss to coat evenly with the sour cream mixture. Season with salt and pepper and refrigerate until needed.

2 To make the sandwiches, butter the bread to the edges, top with the lettuce leaves and cut each slice in half.

3 Leaving one curl of lettuce visible on each slice, spoon the herring salad over the lettuce. Arrange three slices of egg on each sandwich.

4 Season the sandwich with salt and pepper. Garnish each sandwich by tucking a parsley sprig under the egg slices.

Per portion Energy 346kcal/1437kJ; Protein 13.5g; Carbohydrate 15.4g, of which sugars 9.7g; Fat 25.9g, of which saturates 12.5g; Cholesterol 165mg; Calcium 114mg; Fibre 1.6g; Sodium 506mg.

Potatoes with leeks and herring
Kartofler med porrer og spege sild

Some might call this smørrebrød a poor peasant's sandwich given its humble ingredients, but the opposite is true. The first new potatoes are celebrated with gusto throughout Scandinavia, generally with heaps of creamy butter. Although unknown in the far north before the 18th century, potatoes are now an essential part of the traditional Danish diet, and almost no hot meal is served without them. Select the best quality potatoes you can find for this sandwich.

1 Melt 15g/½ oz/1 tbsp of the butter in a frying pan. Stir in the leeks and cook over a medium heat for about 5 minutes, until wilted. Remove from the heat and leave to cool.

2 Spread the slices of bread to the edges with the remaining butter, top with the lettuce leaves and cut each slice in half. Layer 4–6 slices of potato over the lettuce on each sandwich.

3 Arrange 3–4 herring pieces down the centre of the potatoes and spoon 30ml/ 2 tbsp leeks over the herring on each sandwich. Sprinkle with chopped chives.

Per portion Energy 196kcal/819kJ; Protein 6.6g; Carbohydrate 17.2g, of which sugars 4.2g; Fat 11.5g, of which saturates 5.3g; Cholesterol 32mg; Calcium 27mg; Fibre 1.7g; Sodium 347mg.

Makes 4

40g/1½ oz/3 tbsp salted butter, softened

90g/3½ oz leek, sliced

2 slices rye bread

2 round (butterhead) lettuce leaves

4-5 small new potatoes, peeled, boiled and thinly sliced

12–16 pieces Pickled Herring, about 2.5cm/1in square

10ml/2 tsp chopped chives

Cook's tip After the bread has been sliced, move the slices to a serving plate or individual plates before arranging the toppings and garnish.

Smoked salmon with dill and lemon
Røget laks på franskbrød

Smoked salmon is a delicacy in Denmark. Now primarily farm-raised in Norway or Scotland, thin slices of the succulent pink fish are a favourite smørrebrød topping. So as not to compete with the salmon's rich flavour, crusty white bread, or what Danes call franskbrød, is the preferred choice for this smørrebrød. The crusts are left on the bread, and a drizzle of mustard sauce with dill and lemon slices are the traditional garnishes.

1 First make the mustard sauce. In a small bowl, mix together the vinegar, sugar, mustard, egg yolk (if using) and oil. Stir in 7.5ml/1½ tsp chopped dill, and season.

2 Butter the slices of bread to the edges, top with the lettuce leaves and cut each slice in half. Leaving one curl of lettuce visible on each slice, arrange a slice of salmon on each sandwich, folding or rolling the edges to fit.

3 Spoon 5ml/1 tsp mustard sauce down the middle of each sandwich. Cut each lemon slice in half, twist and place in the middle of the salmon. Tuck a dill sprig under each lemon twist.

Per portion Energy 249kcal/1037kJ; Protein 9.3g; Carbohydrate 15.7g, of which sugars 8.9g; Fat 17g, of which saturates 6.2g; Cholesterol 30mg; Calcium 44mg; Fibre 0.3g; Sodium 1265mg.

Makes 4

25g/1oz/2 tbsp salted butter, softened

2 slices crusty white bread

2 round (butterhead) lettuce leaves

4 (100g/3–4 oz) slices smoked salmon

2 lemon slices

4 dill sprigs

For the mustard sauce

15ml/1 tbsp distilled white vinegar

25g/1oz/2 tbsp sugar

90ml/6 tbsp Dijon mustard

1 egg yolk (optional)

50ml/2fl oz/¼ cup vegetable oil

7.5ml/1½ tsp chopped fresh dill

salt and ground black pepper

Cook's tip A layer of thinly sliced cucumber can be substituted for the lettuce leaves.

Makes 4

4 eggs

15ml/1 tbsp milk

40g/1½oz/3 tbsp salted butter, softened

2 slices crusty white bread

2 round (butterhead) lettuce leaves

8 (100g/3oz) slices smoked salmon, depending on size

1 lemon slice, cut into quarters

10ml/2 tsp chopped chives

salt and ground black pepper

Smoked salmon with scrambled eggs
Røget laks med røræg på franskbrød

Thinly sliced smoked salmon is layered over scrambled eggs in this topping, which is particularly popular at smørrebrød *parties on slices of crusty white bread. You could garnish these sandwiches with dill sprigs or pairs of pencil-thin asparagus spears instead of chives if you prefer.*

1 Whisk together the eggs and milk in a small bowl and season with salt and pepper. Melt 15g/½oz/1 tbsp of the butter in a pan over a medium heat.

2 Stir the eggs into the melted butter. Cook, stirring constantly, for 3–4 minutes, until the eggs are softly scrambled. Remove from the heat and leave to cool.

3 Spread the slices of bread to the edges with the remaining butter, top with the lettuce leaves and cut each slice in half. Leaving one curl of lettuce visible on each slice, spoon one quarter of the scrambled eggs over each sandwich.

4 Arrange the smoked salmon to cover the eggs completely, folding or pleating the slices if necessary to fit the bread. Garnish each sandwich with a quarter-slice of lemon, tucked into a fold of the salmon and a sprinkling of chives.

Per portion Energy 316kcal/1314kJ; Protein 22.8g; Carbohydrate 6.6g, of which sugars 0.8g; Fat 22.4g, of which saturates 8.2g; Cholesterol 249mg; Calcium 68mg; Fibre 0.3g; Sodium 231mg.

Makes 4

1 egg

50g/2oz/½ cup fine breadcrumbs

225g/8oz plaice fillets

40g/1½oz/3 tbsp salted butter, softened

2 slices crusty white bread

2 round (butterhead) lettuce leaves

4 lemon slices and 4 fresh dill sprigs

For the remoulade

250ml/8fl oz/1 cup mayonnaise

120ml/4fl oz/½ cup chopped sweet dill pickles or relish

15ml/1 tbsp mustard powder

15ml/1 tbsp finely chopped fresh dill

30ml/2 tbsp finely chopped parsley

30ml/2 tbsp diced onion

2.5ml/½ tsp lemon juice

15ml/1 tbsp capers (optional)

Fried plaice fillet with remoulade
Fiskefilet med remoulade

Danes adore remoulade. A tangy, creamy mayonnaise-based relish with pickles, similar to tartare sauce, this versatile condiment is eaten with seafood, open sandwiches and frikadeller *(Danish meatballs), and used as a garnish or a spread. It is superb as a garnish for fried plaice.*

1 First make the remoulade. Put the mayonnaise in a bowl and stir in the dill pickles or relish, mustard powder, dill, parsley, onion, lemon juice and capers (if using) until well blended. Cover and refrigerate until needed.

2 Briefly whisk the egg with 5ml/1 tsp water in a shallow dish. Place the breadcrumbs in another shallow dish. If required, cut the fillet into four 10–15cm/ 4–6in pieces. Dip the plaice fillet into the egg, then into the breadcrumbs, evenly coating both sides.

3 Melt 15g/½oz/1 tbsp of the butter in a pan over a medium heat, and cook the fillets for about 6 minutes, turning once, until golden brown on each side. Drain on kitchen paper and leave to cool.

4 Spread the slices of bread to the edges with the remaining butter. Place a lettuce leaf on each slice and cut the slices in half. Leaving one curl of lettuce visible on each sandwich, arrange the fish on the lettuce, dividing the pieces evenly. Garnish each sandwich with a spoonful of remoulade, a lemon slice and a sprig of dill.

Per portion Energy 667kcal/2762kJ; Protein 15.6g; Carbohydrate 19.1g, of which sugars 2.3g; Fat 59.9g, of which saturates 12.9g; Cholesterol 140mg; Calcium 89mg; Fibre 0.7g; Sodium 593mg.

Shooting star
Stjerne skud

One of the more fancifully named open sandwiches, this features poached and fried plaice. The delicate flavours of the fish are enhanced by salty caviar.

1 Whisk the egg with 5ml/1 tsp water in a shallow dish. Place the breadcrumbs in another shallow dish. Cut the fillet into eight small 10cm/4in pieces. Dip half the plaice fillets into the egg, then into the breadcrumbs, evenly coating both sides.

2 Melt 15g/½oz/1 tbsp of the butter in a pan over a medium heat and fry the fillets for about 6 minutes, turning once, until golden brown on each side. Lift out the fish and leave to cool. Place the wine and lemon juice in a pan with 50ml/2fl oz/¼ cup water, and bring to a simmer. Add the remaining plaice fillets and poach for 2–3 minutes. Drain.

3 Spread the slices of bread with butter. Place a lettuce leaf on each slice and cut in half. Arrange both the fried and the poached fish over the lettuce, dividing the pieces evenly. Divide the prawns among the sandwiches and arrange in the centre on top of the fish. Place two asparagus spears across the prawns. Spoon 2.5ml/½ tsp caviar in the middle of the prawns and garnish with parsley and lemon.

Per portion Energy 225kcal/944kJ; Protein 18.1g; Carbohydrate 13.9g, of which sugars 1.1g; Fat 11.2g, of which saturates 5.8g; Cholesterol 144mg; Calcium 85mg; Fibre 0.8g; Sodium 377mg.

Makes 4

1 egg

5ml/1 tsp water

35g/1½oz/¾ cup fine breadcrumbs

225g/8oz plaice fillets

40g/1½oz/3 tbsp salted butter, softened

15ml/1 tbsp white wine

5ml/1 tsp lemon juice

2 slices crusty white bread

2 round (butterhead) lettuce leaves

100g/3¾oz small cooked prawns (shrimp)

8 small cooked asparagus spears

10ml/2 tsp lumpfish caviar

4 parsley sprigs

4 lemon slices

Prawns with egg and cucumber

Rejemad med æg og agurkesalat

The icy waters around Greenland, a Danish province since the Viking era, are the preferred source for the sweet, wild prawns in this classic open sandwich, which is always one of the most popular on smørrebrød *menus. Heap the prawns over the lettuce or arrange them in orderly rows according to your style, and how hungry you are!*

1 Butter the slices of bread to the edges, top with the lettuce leaves and cut each slice in half. Place 3 slices of egg toward the top of each lettuce leaf, leaving the top curl visible. Divide the prawns among the sandwiches and arrange them over the rest of the lettuce, partly covering the egg slices.

2 To garnish, top the prawns with a spoonful of mayonnaise and place a dill sprig in the centre of the mayonnaise.

3 Stack two cucumber slices with one lemon slice between them; cut the stack halfway across, and twist to form a curl. Repeat with the remaining cucumber and lemon. Place a cucumber-lemon twist on or beside each sandwich.

Per portion Energy 256kcal/1066kJ; Protein 17.6g; Carbohydrate 6.4g, of which sugars 0.5g; Fat 18.1g, of which saturates 5.5g; Cholesterol 264mg; Calcium 90mg; Fibre 0.2g; Sodium 337mg.

Makes 4

25g/1oz/2 tbsp salted butter, softened

2 slices crusty white bread

2 round (butterhead) lettuce leaves

2 hard-boiled eggs, sliced

300g/11oz/2 cups small cooked prawns (shrimp)

mayonnaise

4 dill sprigs

8 cucumber slices

4 lemon slices

Cook's tip Tomato can be used as a garnish instead of cucumber. If using tomato slices, change the lemon slices to lemon wedges for eye appeal. The egg slices can be placed on top of the prawns, topped with mayonnaise.

25g/1oz/2 tbsp salted butter, softened

2 slices rye bread

2 leaves round (butterhead) lettuce

8 thin slices (125g/4¼oz) cooked ham

12 slices cucumber

4 parsley sprigs

For the Italian salad

115g/4oz/1 cup chopped carrots

115/4oz/1 cup fresh or frozen peas

50ml/2fl oz/¼ cup mayonnaise

5ml/1tsp lemon juice

10ml/2 tsp chopped dill

salt and white pepper

Cook's tip Instead of butter, spread the bread with remoulade.

Ham with Italian salad
Skinke med Italiensk salat

The Danes love all pork products and a wide variety of ham is sold ready-cooked in stores. Garnished with another favourite, a simple pea and carrot combination known in Denmark as Italian salad, this ham sandwich is fresh and satisfying. You need to make the salad in advance.

1 To make the Italian salad place the carrots in a pan with 50ml/2fl oz/¼ cup water. Bring to the boil and cook for 4–5 minutes until nearly tender. Stir in the peas and cook for 2 more minutes. Drain the vegetables, refresh under cold running water, drain again and place in a bowl.

2 Leave the vegetables to cool completely, then stir in the mayonnaise, lemon juice and dill and season with salt and pepper. Chill until needed.

3 To make the sandwiches, butter the slices of bread to the edges, top with the lettuce leaves and cut each slice in half.

4 Leaving one curl of lettuce visible on each piece, pleat or fan two slices of ham over the lettuce. Top the ham on each sandwich with 15ml/1 tbsp Italian salad. Garnish with cucumber slices and parsley sprigs.

Per portion Energy 231kcal/959kJ; Protein 9.4g; Carbohydrate 12.3g, of which sugars 3.8g; Fat 16.4g, of which saturates 5.2g; Cholesterol 41mg; Calcium 30mg; Fibre 2.8g; Sodium 550mg.

Makes 4

40g/1½oz/3 tbsp salted butter, softened

4 button mushrooms, sliced

4 cooked unsmoked streaky (fatty) bacon rashers (strips)

300g/11oz block of Liver Pâté

2 slices rye bread

2 leaves round (butterhead) lettuce

2 slices Pickled Beetroot (beet), cut into matchsticks

parsley, to garnish

Cook's tip Garnish with small pickled gherkins to accent the sandwich's textures and flavours. Small, whole beetroot slices can also be used as a garnish.

Liver pâté with bacon and mushrooms
Leverpostej med bacon og champaignons

One of the most popular smørrebrød *toppings of all in Denmark, liver pâté demonstrates its flavoursome versatility paired with crisp bacon rashers and sautéed mushrooms. Traditionally, the rye bread would have been spread with bacon fat or lard to enhance the rich, earthy taste of the pork liver pâté.*

1 Melt 15g/½oz/1 tbsp of the butter in a frying pan over a medium heat. Stir in the mushrooms and cook for 4–5 minutes, until lightly browned. Remove from the pan and leave to cool.

2 Place the bacon in a frying pan over a medium heat. Cook until browned and crisp. Drain on kitchen paper.

3 Cut the liver pâté into slices with a sharp knife. How thick you cut the slice depends on how much you want, but aim for a thickness of around 5mm/¼in.

4 Spread the slices of bread to the edges with the remaining butter. Place a lettuce leaf on each slice and cut the slices in half. Leaving one curl of lettuce visible, arrange two slices of liver pâté on the lettuce on each slice.

5 Place two slices of bacon over the pâté. Garnish each sandwich with two or three sticks of beetroot and chopped parsley.

Per portion Energy 418kcal/1731kJ; Protein 15g; Carbohydrate 7.8g, of which sugars 1.7g; Fat 36.6g, of which saturates 13.5g; Cholesterol 157mg; Calcium 35mg; Fibre 2.2g; Sodium 868mg.

The veterinarian's evening sandwich
Dyrlægens natmad

The tale behind this classic open sandwich dates from the 1880s and involves a Copenhagen veterinarian who visited the Oskar Davidsen smørrebrød restaurant every day for a breakfast sandwich. He faithfully returned each evening for another. For both meals, his favourite smørrebrød combination included liver pâté and boiled beef with a garnish of beef aspic and sweet onions. The beef aspic needs to be given time to set before you can use it.

1 Make the beef aspic at least 2 hours before you need it. Pour the boiling water into a small bowl. Add the stock cube and gelatine, and stir until both are dissolved. Add the sherry. Pour the mixture into a small, shallow rectangular dish and chill for about 2 hours, until set.

2 To make the sandwiches, butter the bread to the edges and cut the slices in half. Arrange 8–10 watercress leaves on top of each piece of bread.

3 Place two slices of liver pâté on one half of the bread, and two slices of pastrami on the other half, cutting or folding them to fit.

4 Chop the beef aspic into 5mm/¼in cubes and place 4–5 cubes on top of the meats on each sandwich. Arrange four onion rings over the aspic cubes and garnish with a slice of tomato.

Per portion Energy 373kcal/1545kJ; Protein 16.1g; Carbohydrate 8.1g, of which sugars 1.9g; Fat 30.9g, of which saturates 10.8g; Cholesterol 158mg; Calcium 33mg; Fibre 0.9g; Sodium 1019mg.

Makes 4

25g/1oz/2 tbsp salted butter, softened

2 slices rye bread

small bunch watercress, thick stalks removed

8 slices Liver Pâté, 5mm/¼in thick (about 300g/11oz total weight)

8 thin slices deli pastrami (about 115g/4oz total weight)

16 small sweet onion rings

4 tomato slices, seeded

For the beef aspic

250ml/8fl oz/1 cup boiling water

1 beef stock (bouillon) cube

1 sachet (15ml/1 tbsp) powdered gelatine

15ml/1 tbsp dry sherry

Pork fillet with crispy onion rings
Mørbrad Bøf med Bløde Løg

Here, tender roast pork is garnished with two other Danish favourites – the much-loved remoulade, and delicious crispy onion rings – to make this traditional open sandwich.

1 Preheat oven to 190°C/375°F/Gas 5. Place the pork fillet on to a rack in a roasting pan. Season with salt and pepper. Place the pork in a preheated oven and cook until the meat is no longer pink and juices are clear, or the internal temperature reaches 70°C/160°F, about 1 hour. Allow the pork to rest for 15 minutes before slicing 16 slices about 5mm/¼ in thick.

2 Meanwhile, make the crispy onion rings. Pour the buttermilk into a bowl and season with salt and pepper. Add the onion rings, tossing to coat evenly, and leave to soak for about 10 minutes, then drain, discarding the buttermilk.

3 Place the flour in a shallow bowl. Dip the onion rings in the flour to coat them on all sides. Shake off any excess flour. Heat the oil in a frying pan. Fry the onion rings, in batches, over a medium-high heat until golden brown. Drain on kitchen paper.

4 Butter the slices of bread to the edges, top with the lettuce leaves and cut each slice in half. Arrange four pork slices on each sandwich. Arrange 5–6 crispy onion rings over the pork on each sandwich, and garnish with 5ml/1 tsp remoulade, a slice of tomato and a parsley sprig.

Per portion Energy 460kcal/1911kJ; Protein 24.5g; Carbohydrate 20.1g, of which sugars 3.9g; Fat 31.8g, of which saturates 7.5g; Cholesterol 82mg; Calcium 50mg; Fibre 1.8g; Sodium 218mg.

Makes 4

1 pork fillet (tenderloin), about 400g/14oz–600g/1lb 6oz

25g/1oz/2 tbsp salted butter, softened

2 slices rye bread

2 leaves round (butterhead) lettuce

20ml/4 tsp remoulade

4 tomato slices

4 parsley sprigs

For the crispy onion rings

250ml/8fl oz/1 cup buttermilk

1 small onion, thinly sliced, rings separated

175g/6oz/1½ cups plain (all-purpose) flour

250ml/8fl oz/1 cup vegetable oil, for frying

salt and white pepper

Cook's tips
• Orange, cucumber or beetroot slices can also be used as garnishes.
• Cooked, sliced pork tenderloin can also be purchased in the deli department of many supermarkets.

8 unsmoked streaky (fatty) bacon rashers (strips)

75g/3oz/1 cup finely chopped onion

2 firm apples, peeled and chopped

25g/1oz/2 tbsp salted butter, softened

2 slices rye bread

2 leaves round (butterhead) lettuce

4 parsley sprigs

Cook's tip Choose crisp, tart eating apples for this recipe.

Bacon with apples
Stegt flæsk med æbler

Apples appear in many savoury dishes in Denmark, from the classic pork loin stuffed with prunes and apples, to poached apple halves filled with currant jelly served as a side dish with roast pork. In this sandwich, the sweet combination of apples and onions mixed with crisp, salty bacon is rich and satisfying.

1 Fry the bacon over a medium-high heat until crisp; drain on kitchen paper, leaving the fat in the pan.

2 Cook the onion in the reserved bacon fat for 5–7 minutes, until transparent but not browned. Add the apples, and continue cooking for about 5 minutes, until tender. Crumble half the bacon into the apple mixture.

3 Butter the slices of bread to the edges, top with the lettuce leaves and cut each slice in half. Leaving one curl of lettuce visible on each piece, spoon the apple and bacon mixture on to the lettuce, dividing it evenly among the sandwiches.

4 Break the four reserved bacon rashers in half, and place two pieces on each sandwich. Garnish with parsley sprigs, and serve warm.

Per portion Energy 215kcal/895kJ; Protein 9.8g; Carbohydrate 13.9g, of which sugars 8g; Fat 13.7g, of which saturates 6.4g; Cholesterol 40mg; Calcium 21mg; Fibre 2g; Sodium 883mg.

Makes 4

350g/12oz fillet steak (beef tenderloin)
25g/1oz/2 tbsp salted butter, softened
2 slices rye bread
32–40 watercress leaves
8 slices Pickled Beetroot (beet)
16 thin slices sweet onion
4 egg yolks
25ml/1½ tbsp capers

Beef tartare with egg yolk, onion and beetroot
Bøf Tartar med æggeblomme, løg og rødbeder

Raw meat may not be to everyone's taste, but beef tartare is a luxury for connoisseurs, and is a sophisticated dish presented on an open sandwich. Contrasting textures and flavours in the garnishes, plus the drama of a raw egg yolk balanced on the tender meat, give this smørrebrød extra flamboyance. Buy the best-quality well hung fillet steak (beef tenderloin) you can find.

1 Slice the fillet steak into very thin slices. You will find this easier if you first place the fillet in the freezer for 5–8 minutes first. Use a very sharp knife.

2 Butter the slices of bread to the edges, and cut the slices in half. Arrange 8–10 watercress leaves in a fan shape at the top of each slice.

3 Place the beef slices on the bread, overlapping the watercress, layering or folding the slices as needed and extending over the bread.

4 Arrange two slices of beetroot on each sandwich and four onion rings over the beetroot. Carefully place an egg yolk on each sandwich, centering it in an onion ring to keep it in place. Sprinkle with capers.

Per portion Energy 291kcal/1215kJ; Protein 22.1g; Carbohydrate 11g, of which sugars 4.8g; Fat 18g, of which saturates 7.7g; Cholesterol 258mg; Calcium 56mg; Fibre 1.8g; Sodium 201mg.

Cook's tips
• Separate the egg yolk when you need it. So there is less chance of it breaking, simply transfer the yolk from the eggshell onto the sandwich.
• Substitute hollandaise sauce for the egg yolk.

Roast beef, remoulade, crispy onions and horseradish

Roastbeef, remoulade, ristede løg og peberrod

Thinly sliced roast beef with horseradish is a delicious combination and in this sandwich, remoulade, and crispy onions give added texture and flavour. Use cold cuts from your own beef joint, or buy the meat ready cut.

1 Butter the slices of bread to the edges, top with the lettuce leaves and cut each slice in half. Leaving one curl of lettuce visible on each piece, pleat or fan 2–3 slices of beef over the lettuce.

2 Top each sandwich with two slices of beetroot, 5ml/1 tsp remoulade, a few crispy onion rings and 5ml/1 tsp creamed horseradish.

Per portion Energy 171kcal/711kJ; Protein 8g; Carbohydrate 7.7g, of which sugars 2g; Fat 12.2g, of which saturates 5g; Cholesterol 34mg; Calcium 18mg; Fibre 0.9g; Sodium 205mg.

Serves 4

25g/1oz/2 tbsp salted butter, softened

2 slices rye bread

2 leaves round (butterhead) lettuce

8–12 thin slices roast beef, about 115g–185g/4oz–6 ½oz

8 small slices Pickled Beetroot (beet)

20ml/4 tsp remoulade

Crispy onion rings

20ml/4 tsp creamed horseradish

Cook's tip For the Crispy Onions follow the recipe given with the Pork Fillet sandwich.

Fish & shellfish

Salt cod with mustard sauce

Baked cod with cream

Fried eel with potatoes in cream sauce

Salmon steaks with warm potato salad

Fried salt herring with red onion compote

Fish cakes

Halibut fillets with parsley sauce

Enjoying fish
all year round

Since the first rugged Dane put out to sea centuries ago, fish
have been an important part of the Danish diet and economy,
especially during the bleak winter months. The Skagerrak and
Kattegat Straits, the Baltic Sea, the waters around Bornholm
Island and the North Atlantic Ocean stretching between
Denmark, Iceland and Greenland are open fishing grounds for
the Danish fleet. Add additional species from the west coast
of Norway, a country joined with Denmark for four centuries,
and the range seems unlimited, though history does tell of
erratic seasons when herring shoals disappeared and hunger
really did set in.

The seafood most commonly cooked in Denmark includes
herring, plaice, salmon, cod, herring, halibut, farmed trout, and
shellfish such as crayfish, lobster and Greenland prawns
(shrimp). Eel, a perennial favourite, is caught as it returns from
the ocean to spawn in freshwater streams and lakes.

To preserve the catch, salting, drying, pickling and smoking
techniques were traditionally used and remain popular today
because of their flavoursome results. The technique for drying
cod in the open air was devised by the Vikings, when a stash
of preserved fish enabled these adventurers to make their
extensive sea journeys. The salting of dried cod dates from
medieval times, when Scandinavian merchants exchanged
fish for salt with Mediterranean traders.

In typical Danish style, fish dishes are prepared simply so
the flavours shine through. Dredged in flour and fried in butter,
boiled, baked or poached, the cooking methods are relatively
fast, easy and reliable. Parsley sauce, mustard and dill sauce
or, of course, remoulade are served to add flair and flavour to
these simple dishes.

Salt cod with mustard sauce
Kogt torsk med sennep sovs

Mustard sauce is the traditional accompaniment for salmon, but Danes also enjoy it with this recipe and with other fish dishes. You need to soak the salted fish in plenty of cold water for 48 hours; changing the water several times. After soaking, taste a small piece of the fish to test its salt content – thicker parts may need to be soaked longer. This dish is often served with boiled new potatoes, pickled beetroots, and if desired, grated fresh horseradish for some added pungency.

1 After the cod has been sufficiently soaked, cut it into 4–8 serving-size pieces, and set aside.

2 Fill a large pot with enough water to cover the fish and add the salt, onion, bay leaf, peppercorns, cloves and lemon slices.

3 Bring the stock to the boil, add the fish pieces, lower the heat, cover and simmer until the fish turns opaque and flakes easily with a fork, about 10 minutes.

4 For the mustard sauce, mix together the vinegar, sugar, mustard, egg yolk (if using) and oil. Stir in the chopped fresh dill and season to taste.

5 When the fish is cooked, remove the fish from the broth with a slotted spoon and divide the pieces evenly among four warmed serving plates.

6 Top each serving with 15ml/1 tbsp butter, and generously sprinkle with the chopped hard-boiled egg and parsley. Serve the fish with the mustard sauce, boiled new potatoes and pickled beetroot.

Per portion Energy 570kcal/2387kJ; Protein 70.6g; Carbohydrate 8.8g, of which sugars 8.4g; Fat 28.4g, of which saturates 10.5g; Cholesterol 296mg; Calcium 86mg; Fibre 0g; Sodium 1592mg.

Serves 4

800g/1¾lb dried salt cod, soaked, skin and bones removed

1 litre/1¾ pints/4 cups water

30ml/2 tbsp salt

1 onion, sliced

1 bay leaf

10 whole peppercorns

4 whole cloves

4 lemon slices

60ml/4 tbsp butter

2 hard-boiled eggs, chopped, and chopped parsley to garnish

For the mustard sauce

15ml/1 tbsp distilled white vinegar

25g/1oz/2 tbsp sugar

90ml/6 tbsp Dijon mustard

1 egg yolk (optional)

50ml/2fl oz/¼ cup vegetable oil

7.5ml/1½ tsp chopped fresh dill

salt and ground black pepper

Serves 4–6

1.3kg/3lb cod steaks

15ml/1 tbsp salt

1 egg, beaten

50g/2oz/½ cup fine breadcrumbs

40g/1½oz/3 tbsp butter, cut into small pieces

300ml/½ pint/1¼ cups single (light) cream

45ml/3 tbsp chopped fresh parsley, to garnish

8 lemon wedges, to garnish

Baked cod with cream
Bagt torsk med fløde

Always versatile, cod is enjoyed throughout the year, but baked or poached whole fresh cod is traditionally served in Denmark for dinner on New Year's Eve. The simple preparation shows off the lean, firm texture of the flavoursome white fish. Serve with boiled potatoes, remoulade or mustard sauce and peas.

1 Preheat the oven to 190°C/375°F/Gas 5. Pat the fish steaks dry and rub the salt over the skin. Place in a lightly greased baking dish, brush with the egg, sprinkle with breadcrumbs and dot with butter. Pour the cream around the steaks.

2 Bake the fish for about 15–20 minutes, depending on thickness, until the topping is browned and the flesh flakes easily with a fork. Serve sprinkled with parsley and garnished with lemon wedges.

Per portion Energy 355kcal/1484kJ; Protein 42.5g; Carbohydrate 8.9g, of which sugars 1.4g; Fat 16.7g, of which saturates 9.8g; Cholesterol 141mg; Calcium 78mg; Fibre 0.2g; Sodium 261mg.

Cook's tip If you can find a whole cod, bake it in the oven for around 1 hour, adding the cream 20 minutes before the end of the cooking time.

Fried eel with potatoes in cream sauce
Stegt ål med flødestuvede kartofler

A legacy of Denmark's rural past, fried eel is a choice delicacy. Served with boiled or creamed potatoes and accompanied by icy aquavit and beer, this seasonal dish is a summer speciality.

1 Cut the eel into 10cm/4in lengths. Whisk together the egg and water in a shallow dish. Place the breadcrumbs in a second shallow dish. Dip the eel first into the egg mixture, then into the breadcrumbs to coat both sides evenly. Sprinkle with salt and pepper. Leave the fish to rest for at least 10 minutes.

2 Melt the butter in a large pan over a medium-high heat. Add the eel pieces and cook, turning once, for about 10 minutes on each side, depending on thickness, until the coating is golden brown and the eel is tender. Remove from the pan and drain on kitchen paper. Keep warm.

3 Meanwhile, boil the potatoes in salted water for about 20 minutes. Drain, slice and keep warm. Melt the butter in a pan and stir in the flour. Cook, stirring, for 5 minutes until the roux is pale beige. Slowly stir in the cream and cook for about 5 minutes, stirring constantly, until the sauce has thickened. Season to taste. Stir the potato slices into the cream sauce. Serve with the fried eel, sprinkled with parsley and garnished with lemon wedges.

Per portion Energy 978kcal/4074kJ; Protein 50.2g; Carbohydrate 43.7g, of which sugars 5.6g; Fat 68.2g, of which saturates 32.3g; Cholesterol 483mg; Calcium 184mg; Fibre 2.3g; Sodium 448mg.

Serves 4

1kg/2¼lb eel, skinned and cleaned

1 egg

5ml/1 tsp water

25g/1oz/½ cup fine breadcrumbs, toasted

10ml/2 tsp salt

2.5ml/½ tsp white pepper

40g/1½oz/3 tbsp butter

2 lemons, sliced into wedges, to garnish

For the potatoes

800g/1¾lb potatoes, peeled

5ml/1 tsp salt

40g/1½oz/3 tbsp butter

20g/¾oz/3 tbsp plain (all-purpose) flour

475ml/16fl oz/2 cups single (light) cream

salt and white pepper, to taste

45ml/3 tbsp chopped fresh parsley, to garnish

Cook's tips A balloon whisk will help keep the roux smooth. Look for fresh eel in Asian markets.

Salmon steaks with warm potato salad
Kogt laks med varm kartoffelsalat

Salmon is a favourite fish in Denmark for special occasions, festivals and significant anniversaries. It was once plentiful in the wild, but most of the salmon eaten in Scandinavia today is farmed. Simply poached, salmon's savoury taste shines through, enriched by the wine and lemon juice flavours in the poaching liquid. Warm potato salad is another Danish favourite, and its buttery, tangy dressing complements the salmon. Serve with asparagus.

1 Place the dill sprigs in the bottom of a 23 x 33cm/9 x 13in rectangular baking dish or small fish kettle. Arrange the salmon over the dill or on the tray of a fish kettle. Combine the water with the wine, vinegar or lemon juice and salt and add the allspice berries and bay leaves. Pour over the salmon. Bring the liquid to a simmer, then lower the heat, cover and cook for 10–15 minutes.

2 Peel the potatoes and boil them whole in lightly salted water for 20–25 minutes, until tender. To make the dressing place the onion in a pan with the water. Bring to the boil over a medium-high heat, and cook for about 5 minutes, until the onion is transparent. Stir in the vinegar, sugar and mustard and season to taste with salt and pepper, adding a little more water if necessary. Stir in the butter until melted and keep warm.

3 Drain the potatoes and allow to cool slightly. While they are still warm, cut them into 1cm/½in slices and layer them in a large bowl. Pour over the dressing, add the parsley and toss gently to coat the potatoes evenly.

4 When the fish is opaque and flakes easily with a fork, skim off any scum and lift out the fish, drain and allow to cool slightly. Remove the skin from the salmon before placing on a serving platter or on individual plates. Garnish with dill sprigs and lemon slice twists and serve with the warm potato salad.

Serves 6

3 bunches fresh dill

6 salmon steaks, each about 2.5cm/1in thick (1.3kg/3lb total weight)

475ml/16fl oz/2 cups water

250ml/8fl oz/1 cup dry white wine

15ml/1 tbsp white vinegar or lemon juice

5ml/1 tsp salt

5 whole allspice berries

2 bay leaves

6 small dill sprigs, to garnish

6 lemon slices, to garnish

For the warm potato salad

1.2kg/2½lb potatoes

175g/6oz chopped onion

175ml/6fl oz/¾ cup water

45ml/3 tbsp cider vinegar

10ml/2 tsp caster (superfine) sugar

5ml/1 tsp mustard powder

salt and ground white pepper

25g/1oz/2 tbsp butter

45ml/3 tbsp chopped parsley

Cook's tip Salmon steaks can also be poached in the oven. Preheat the oven to 200°C/400°F/Gas 6. Place the fish and poaching liquid in the kettle and cook for 20–25 minutes.

Per portion Energy 578kcal/2420kJ; Protein 47.6g; Carbohydrate 36.3g, of which sugars 6g; Fat 27.9g, of which saturates 6.5g; Cholesterol 117mg; Calcium 67mg; Fibre 2.4g; Sodium 146mg.

Serves 4

8 salted herring fillets (about 675g/1½lb total weight)

15g/3oz/1½ cup fine breadcrumbs

40g/1½oz/3 tbsp butter

2.5ml/½ tsp white pepper

For the red onion compote

675g/1½lb red onions, diced

75ml/2½fl oz/⅓ cup cider vinegar

350ml/12fl oz/1½ cups red wine

250ml/8fl oz/1 cup water

50ml/2fl oz/¼ cup honey

15ml/1 tbsp soft light brown sugar

10ml/2 tsp butter

salt and ground black pepper

Cook's tips Add 250ml/8fl oz/1 cup single (light) cream to the pan after removing the herring. Cook for 3 minutes over a medium heat, stirring, and pour the sauce over the fish.

Fried salt herring with red onion compote
Stegt sild med rødløgs kompot

By the 12th century, salt herring was a staple food throughout Scandinavia. Although salt was rare and costly in medieval times, it was worth the expense to preserve the seasonal shoals of herring, which arrived along the coast only in late summer. Although other ways of preserving herring have been developed, the Danes have retained a taste for salted fish.

1 Rinse the herring several times in cold water. Place in a bowl of cold water, cover and leave to soak overnight in the refrigerator.

2 Taste the herring for saltiness. If it is too salty, rinse the fillets again. Otherwise, drain, pat dry with kitchen paper and place on a plate.

3 To make the red onion compote, place the chopped onion in a pan and add the vinegar and red wine. Bring to the boil and cook, uncovered, over a medium heat for about 30 minutes, stirring occasionally, until the liquid has evaporated. Stir in the water, honey, brown sugar and butter, and season with salt and pepper. Cook for a further 15 minutes, stirring occasionally, until reduced and thick. Cover and keep warm until needed.

4 Place the breadcrumbs in a shallow dish and dip the herring fillets into the crumbs to coat both sides evenly. Sprinkle with pepper.

5 Melt the butter in a large frying pan over a medium-high heat. Fry the herring fillets, in batches if necessary, turning once, for about 4 minutes on each side, until the coating is golden brown and the fish flakes easily with a fork. Remove the fish from the pan, drain on kitchen paper, and keep warm until all the fillets are cooked.

6 Divide the fillets between four serving plates. Spoon the red onion compote over the fish and serve immediately.

Per portion Energy 672kcal/2805kJ; Protein 35.9g; Carbohydrate 43.5g, of which sugars 23.7g; Fat 34.1g, of which saturates 12.3g; Cholesterol 114mg; Calcium 186mg; Fibre 2.8g; Sodium 460mg.

Serves 4

450g/1lb cod or plaice fillet

225g/8oz salmon fillet

175g/6oz smoked salmon

30ml/2 tbsp finely chopped onion

40g/1½oz/3 tbsp melted butter

3 eggs

25g/1oz/¼ cup plain (all-purpose) flour

salt and white pepper

Fish cakes
Fiskefrikadeller

Baked in the oven, fish cakes are a steadfast favourite throughout Denmark. Serve the fish cakes with remoulade, buttered potatoes and Pickled cucumber salad to make a complete supper.

1 Place the cod and salmon fillets in a shallow dish, and sprinkle with 15ml/1 tbsp salt to draw some of the moisture out. Leave the fish to rest for 10 minutes, then pat dry with kitchen paper.

2 Place the cod and salmon, with the smoked salmon, in a food processor. Add the onion, butter, eggs and flour and pulse until smooth; season with salt and pepper and spoon into a bowl.

3 Preheat the oven to 190°C/375°F/Gas 5. Lightly grease a 23 x 33cm/9 x 13in baking tray. With damp hands, form the fish mixture into 16 slightly flattened, round patties, and place them on the prepared tray.

4 Bake the fish cakes in the preheated oven for 30–35 minutes, until they are cooked through and lightly browned. Serve immediately.

Per portion Energy 407kcal/1700kJ; Protein 48.5g; Carbohydrate 5.5g, of which sugars 0.6g; Fat 21.4g, of which saturates 7.9g; Cholesterol 259mg; Calcium 64mg; Fibre 0.3g; Sodium 1029mg.

Cook's tips Serve the fish cakes with mustard sauce instead of remoulade. Instead of baking they can be fried or grilled (broiled).

Halibut fillets with parsley sauce
Helleflynderkoteletter med Persillesovs

Norsemen considered halibut 'the fish of the gods' and a holy fish, and linked it to Baldur, the wise and kind 'white god'. In Denmark, this traditional dish is often served with steamed cauliflower and buttered new potatoes, but buttered shredded green cabbage or braised leeks would also work well.

1 Cut the halibut into four pieces. Whisk the eggs and water together in a shallow dish. Place the breadcrumbs in a second shallow dish. Dip the fish into the egg mixture, then into the breadcrumbs, to coat both sides evenly. Sprinkle with salt and pepper. Allow the fish to rest at least 10 minutes before cooking.

2 To make the parsley sauce, melt the butter in a pan over a medium heat, and whisk in the flour. Reduce the heat and cook the roux for 3–5 minutes until pale beige. Slowly add the milk into the roux; cook, whisking constantly, for about 5 minutes, until the sauce comes to the boil and becomes smooth and thick. Season, add the parsley and simmer for 2 minutes. Cover and keep warm.

3 Melt the butter in a large pan over a medium-high heat. Place the halibut fillets in the pan, and cook for about 4 minutes on each side, turning once, until the coating is golden brown and the fish flakes easily with a fork. Serve the halibut fillets with the sauce spooned over accompanied by freshly cooked vegetables.

Per portion Energy 594kcal/2493kJ; Protein 58.2g; Carbohydrate 30.4g, of which sugars 5g; Fat 27.6g, of which saturates 14.1g; Cholesterol 227mg; Calcium 234mg; Fibre 0.9g; Sodium 487mg.

Serves 4

900g/2lb halibut fillet

2 eggs, beaten

10ml/2 tsp water

75g/3oz/1½ cup fine breadcrumbs

10ml/2 tsp salt

2.5ml/½ tsp white pepper

50g/2oz/4 tbsp butter

4 lemon wedges, to garnish

For the parsley sauce

50g/2oz/4 tbsp butter

60ml/4 tbsp plain (all-purpose) flour

350ml/12fl oz/1½ cups milk

45ml/3tbsp finely chopped parsley

salt

Meat, poultry & game

Roast pork, crackling and glazed potatoes

Pork loin stuffed with apples and prunes

Mock hare, redcurrant jelly sauce and Hasselback potatoes

Danish meatballs

Easter rack of lamb

Beef patties with onions and fried egg

Venison tenderloins with cherry sauce

Roast duck with prunes and apples

Braised chicken

Roast chicken with lingonberries

Plump pigs and chicken on Sunday

Denmark is a true meat-and-potatoes country. While beef, lamb, turkey, veal and chicken are increasingly popular, pork still tops the list as a Dane's favourite meat. Hearty, succulent and satisfying, pork in one of its many forms, served with gravy and some variation of potato, is the Danish idea of a perfect meal. Roast pork with crackling and Pork loin stuffed with prunes and apples are both classic dishes enjoyed on special occasions during autumn and winter.

For weeknight meals, minced (ground) pork, sometimes blended with beef or veal, is made into meatballs, often dubbed the national dish, or a simple meatloaf. Beef patties with onions, sometimes topped with a fried egg, is one of Denmark's oldest workers' lunch dishes.

At Easter, a glorious crown of roast lamb is served at many family gatherings, and succulent venison tenderloins are popular during the winter months. On Christmas Eve, a plump, stuffed roast goose or duck with stuffed with prunes and apples is the star attraction.

Chicken is also a traditional dish, but one that took a while to achieve acceptance. When Denmark's farm co-operative movement started, chickens were reserved for egg production, considered a more economical use of resources. For decades, the actual bird was expensive and eaten only on special occasions. Even though chicken is more affordable today in Denmark, the delicious chicken for Sunday supper tradition continues.

Roast pork, crackling and glazed potatoes

Flæskesteg med svær og sukkerbrunede kartofler

Pork is the favourite meat in Denmark, and roast pork with golden crackling is a much-loved dish, especially during winter. For this recipe, select a bone-in pork loin with the skin left on for the crackling.

1 Preheat the oven to 200°C/400°F/Gas 6. Use a sharp knife to score the pork skin with diagonal cuts to make a diamond pattern. Rub the rind with the salt, pepper and mustard powder. Push the cloves and bay leaves into the skin.

2 Place the pork loin, skin side up, on a rack in a roasting pan and cook for about 1 hour, until the skin is crisp and golden. Pour the water into the bottom of the roasting pan and cook for a further 30 minutes.

3 Boil the potatoes in salted water for 15–20 minutes, or until soft. Drain, peel and keep warm. Melt the sugar in a frying pan over a low heat until it turns light brown. Add the potatoes and butter, stirring to coat the potatoes, and cook for about 6–8 minutes, until the potatoes are a rich golden brown. Keep warm.

4 To cook the apples, bring the water to the boil in a large pan and stir in the brown sugar. Add the lemon juice and apple halves, lower the heat and poach gently until the apples are just tender. Remove the apples from the pan. Spoon 7.5ml/1½ tsp redcurrant jelly into the hollow of each apple half and keep warm.

5 When the pork is cooked, transfer it to a serving dish and leave it in a warm place to rest for 15 minutes before carving. Meanwhile, make the gravy; transfer the roasting pan juices into a pan and reduce over a medium heat. Whisk in a little cream if you wish, and season with salt and pepper to taste.

6 Remove the crackling from the pork, and serve it separately, warm. Serve the pork with the gravy, caramelized potatoes and poached apple halves.

Serves 8–10

1 bone-in pork loin, weighing about 2.25kg/5lb

10ml/2 tsp mustard powder

15 whole cloves

2 bay leaves

900ml/1½ pints/3¾ cups water

175ml/6fl oz/¾ cup single (light) cream (optional)

salt and white pepper

Braised red cabbage, to serve

For the glazed potatoes

900g/2lb small potatoes

50g/2oz/¼ cup caster (superfine) sugar

65g/2½ oz/5 tbsp butter

For the apples with redcurrant jelly

750ml/1¼ pints/3 cups water

115g/4oz/generous ½ cup soft light brown sugar

5ml/1 tsp lemon juice

4–5 tart apples, peeled, cored and halved

60–75ml/4–5 tbsp redcurrant jelly

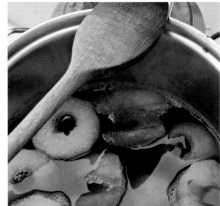

Per portion Energy 654kcal/2735kJ; Protein 36.9g; Carbohydrate 39.5g, of which sugars 26.2g; Fat 39.9g, of which saturates 16.1g; Cholesterol 124mg; Calcium 36mg; Fibre 1.5g; Sodium 152mg.

Pork loin stuffed with apples and prunes
Mørbrad med æbler og svesker

The centrepiece of many autumn and winter meals, this simple yet elegant pork roast is another showcase for Danish pork. After developing the breed over decades, Danish farmers now have a pig that is sleek and succulent. The result is flavoursome, lean and tender pork. Stuffed with a sweet prune and apple filling, the boneless loin in this recipe is deceptively easy to prepare for a sophisticated result. Complete this classic Danish feast with Glazed potatoes, Braised red cabbage, redcurrant jelly and cold beer.

1 Place the prunes in a pan, cover with water, and bring to the boil over a high heat. Cook briefly, then remove from the heat, and leave to cool for 30 minutes. Drain the prunes, discarding the liquid, and set aside. Peel, core and dice the apples. Place them in a bowl and toss with the lemon juice.

2 Use a long, sharp knife to cut a deep slit lengthwise along the pork joint, starting and ending 2.5cm/1in from each end. Open the pocket and season with salt and pepper. Stuff the joint with the prunes and apples, alternating them down the length of the pocket, and sprinkle the fruit with sugar. Using fine string, tie the meat at 2.5cm/1in intervals to close and secure the pocket.

3 Preheat the oven to 180°C/350°F/Gas 4. Place the butter and vegetable oil in a large flameproof pot with a lid and heat over a medium heat. Place the pork in the pot and cook for about 20 minutes, turning frequently, until browned on all sides.

4 Pour in the stock or water and bring to a simmer. Cover the pot and place in the oven. Cook for about 2 hours until the meat is tender and cooked through. Remove from the oven and leave to rest for 5 minutes.

5 Skim off excess fat from the pan juices and bring them to the boil over a high heat. Stir in the flour, then the redcurrant jelly, reduce the heat to medium, and continue to stir while simmering to make a smooth sauce. Serve with the pork, carved into 2.5cm/1in thick slices.

Serves 6–8

12–14 pitted prunes

2 large, tart eating apples

10ml/2 tsp lemon juice

2.25kg/5lb boneless loin of pork

5ml/1 tsp sugar

25g/1oz/2 tbsp butter

30ml/2 tbsp vegetable oil

250ml/8fl oz/1 cup beef stock or water

15ml/1tbsp plain (all-purpose) flour

250ml/8fl oz/1 cup redcurrant jelly

salt and ground black pepper

Cook's tip To make sure the stuffing is in the centre of the meat, first tie up the loin at 2.5cm/1in intervals with fine string. Use a long, sharp knife or a sharpening steel to force a hole through the loin from each end, turning it to make an opening at least 2cm/¾in in diameter. Use your fingers or the handle of a wooden spoon to force the apples and prunes alternately into the hole. Push them through from both sides so they meet in the middle, making sure there are no gaps. Cook the loin as directed above.

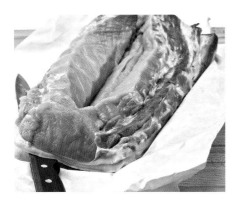

Per portion Energy 610kcal/2566kJ; Protein 76.3g; Carbohydrate 33.8g, of which sugars 32.3g; Fat 19.7g, of which saturates 7.6g; Cholesterol 202mg; Calcium 47mg; Fibre 1.9g; Sodium 184mg.

Serves 6

450g/1lb lean minced (ground) beef

450g/1lb minced (ground) pork

75g/3oz/1½ cups fine breadcrumbs

25g/1oz/2 tbsp finely chopped onion

2 eggs

75ml/5 tbsp/double (heavy) cream

3–4 streaky (fatty) bacon rashers (strips)

salt and ground black pepper

For the Hasselback potatoes

12 medium-sized oval or round potatoes (about 1.8kg/4 lb total weight)

50g/2oz/¼ cup butter

25g/1oz/½ cup fine breadcrumbs

25g/1oz/⅓ cup freshly grated Parmesan cheese

salt and white pepper

For the sauce

15g/½oz/1 tbsp butter

25g/1oz/¼ cup plain (all-purpose) flour

120ml/4fl oz/½ cup single (light) cream

60ml/4 tbsp redcurrant jelly

salt and white pepper

Cook's tip To avoid slicing through the potatoes, place against the edge of a chopping board about 8mm/⅜in thick, and cut to the level of the board.

Mock hare, redcurrant jelly sauce and Hasselback potatoes
Forloren hare med ribs gele og Hasselback kartofler

This hearty meatloaf is intended to imitate hare or rabbit. Served with gravy subtly sweetened with redcurrant jelly, along with buttery fans of Hasselback potatoes, the meatloaf makes a rich meal with luxurious flavours.

1 Preheat the oven to 190°C/375°F/Gas 5. Put the minced beef and pork in a bowl and mix together thoroughly. Stir in the breadcrumbs, onion, eggs, cream, salt and pepper. Turn the mixture into a 12.5 x 23cm/5 x 9in loaf tin (pan), pressing it in firmly, and arrange the bacon rashers over the top. Bake for 1 hour.

2 Meanwhile, lightly grease a baking dish. Peel the potatoes and rinse under cold water. Cut each potato crossways into 8–10 thin, even slices, taking care not to cut all the way through to the bottom, so the slices hold together.

3 Place the potatoes, sliced side up, in the prepared baking dish. Dot evenly with butter, and sprinkle with salt and pepper. Roast for about 1–1½ hours, or until tender and light brown, basting with butter during cooking. Sprinkle with breadcrumbs and grated cheese 20 minutes before the end of the cooking time.

4 When the meatloaf is cooked through, pour off the fat and reserve. Leave the loaf to cool for 15 minutes while you make the sauce. Pour 75ml/2½fl oz/⅓ cup of reserved fat into a pan, add the butter and heat until it melts. Whisk in the flour, and cook, stirring, for 2–4 minutes until well blended. Stir in the cream, redcurrant jelly, salt and pepper. Cook until smooth and heated through.

5 Slice the meatloaf and serve drizzled with the redcurrant sauce and accompanied by the Hasselback potatoes.

Per portion Energy 935kcal/3903kJ; Protein 41.2g; Carbohydrate 69.2g, of which sugars 12.1g; Fat 56.7g, of which saturates 28.6g; Cholesterol 199mg; Calcium 136mg; Fibre 3.5g; Sodium 478mg.

Danish meatballs
Frikadeller

Some say this is the national dish of Denmark. Traditionally served in Danish homes at least once a week, it's a recipe every cook knows in two or three versions. When eaten for the evening meal, frikadeller are served with gravy, boiled potatoes and pickles, or eaten with rye bread, red cabbage and sliced dill pickles. The Danes always peel their boiled potatoes after cooking, but if you prefer, leave the skins on.

1 In a small bowl, beat the eggs well. In a separate, larger bowl, mix the minced veal, minced pork, breadcrumbs and chopped onion together until well blended. Mix in the beaten egg. You might find it easier to use your hands rather than a spoon to blend the ingredients properly.

2 Add the milk, salt and pepper to the bowl and continue mixing until all the ingredients are thoroughly blended to make a soft, moist mixture. Refrigerate the mixture for 15–30 minutes, or until you are ready to cook the meatballs; this will help you to shape it into balls.

3 Melt the butter in a large frying pan over a medium heat. Use two spoons to form 16–20 oval patties about 4cm/1½in across: scoop the meat mixture with one spoon and use the second to slide the patty into the pan.

4 Cook the meatballs for 8–10 minutes, in batches of four or five if necessary, turning once, until the patties are golden brown. Cut one to check that the meat is not pink in the centre. Remove the cooked meatballs from the pan and drain on kitchen paper. Keep warm until all the meatballs are cooked. Serve immediately.

Serves 4

2 eggs

225g/8oz minced (ground) veal

225g/8oz minced (ground) pork

25g/1oz/½ cup fine breadcrumbs

40g/1½oz/½ cup finely chopped onion

250ml/8fl oz/1 cup milk

75ml/3oz/6 tbsp butter

salt and ground black pepper

Cook's tip Make a double batch of meatballs and freeze them, uncooked, for up to three months. You can also freeze them after they are fried, and then reheat them in the oven. When rolled into much smaller balls, the meatballs are often served at parties as finger food, with pickles.

Per portion Energy 404kcal/1683kJ; Protein 28.4g; Carbohydrate 8.7g, of which sugars 3.8g; Fat 28.8g, of which saturates 14.9g; Cholesterol 211mg; Calcium 112mg; Fibre 0.3g; Sodium 307mg.

Easter rack of lamb
Påske lam

Gathering with family members and sharing an Easter feast featuring a magnificent rack of lamb, simply cooked, marks the holiday for many Danes. Accompany the roast lamb and vegetables with steamed asparagus and lingonberry sauce.

1 Preheat the oven to 220°C/425°F/Gas 7. To prepare the meat, make a slit in the membrane on each rib and arrange the racks in a circle with the bone ends curving outward.

2 Tie the ribs with fine string to secure them in the crown position. (You can ask your butcher to prepare the crown roast for you.) Wrap the bone ends with foil to prevent them from burning. Rub the meat with salt and pepper, and place the crown on a rack in a roasting pan.

3 Place the lamb in the preheated oven and immediately lower the temperature to 180°C/350°F/Gas 4. Roast for 1½ hours. Do not cover or baste while cooking.

4 Remove the pan from the oven and arrange the potatoes, onions and carrots around the base of the crown. Cook for about 30 minutes more, or until the meat is done to your liking and the vegetables are tender.

5 Transfer the lamb and vegetables to a serving dish and keep warm. Skim the fat from the pan juices. To make the gravy, pour 45ml/3 tbsp pan juices into a pan over a medium heat.

6 Whisk the flour into the pan juices and cook for 3–4 minutes until the flour is absorbed. Slowly stir in the remaining pan juices and the stock; cook until thickened. Season to taste with salt and pepper.

Serves 8–10

1.8–2kg/4–4½lb rack of lamb, fat trimmed from bones

900g/2lb red potatoes, peeled and halved

3 medium onions, quartered

900g/2lb carrots, halved lengthways

40g/1½oz/⅓ cup plain (all-purpose) flour

250ml/8fl oz/1 cup good lamb stock

salt and ground black pepper

chopped parsley, to garnish

Cook's tips

• When purchasing a rack of lamb, calculate four to five ribs per person, depending on the size of the lamb.

• For medium-rare lamb, allow 60 minutes per kilogram/30 minutes per pound cooking time; for medium lamb, allow 70 minutes per kilogram/35 minutes per pound.

Per portion Energy 493kcal/2050kJ; Protein 25.6g; Carbohydrate 28.7g, of which sugars 10.7g; Fat 31.5g, of which saturates 15.1g; Cholesterol 97mg; Calcium 62mg; Fibre 3.9g; Sodium 113mg.

450g/1lb lean minced (ground) beef

45ml/3 tbsp breadcrumbs

20g/¾oz/¼ cup finely chopped onions

1 egg

15g/½oz/¼ cup chopped parsley

120ml/4fl oz/½ cup milk

65g/2½oz/5 tbsp butter

3 medium onions, sliced

4 eggs

salt and ground black pepper

Beef patties with onions and fried egg
Hakkebøf med bløde løg

Fried beef patties are a very old, traditional Danish dish, a workers' meal still enjoyed today all around the country. Most often served for lunch, the patties are served with buttered flat bread and pickled red cabbage or gherkins.

1 Put the beef in a mixing bowl, add the breadcrumbs, chopped onion, egg and parsley and mix well. Gradually stir in the milk until thoroughly blended to make a soft, moist mixture. Season with salt and pepper. Refrigerate for 15–30 minutes.

2 Melt 40g/1½oz/3 tbsp of the butter in a pan over a medium heat. Divide the meat mixture into four and form rounded patties. Place in the pan and cook for 8–10 minutes, turning once, until browned. Remove from the pan and keep warm.

3 Melt the remaining butter in the pan, add the sliced onions and cook for 6–8 minutes, until soft and golden. When the onions are ready, fry the eggs in a little hot oil in a separate pan.

4 To serve, place the patties on four serving plates and top each with a spoonful of cooked onions. Place a fried egg on the onions and serve immediately.

Per portion Energy 527kcal/2189kJ; Protein 32.7g; Carbohydrate 11.8g, of which sugars 2.9g; Fat 39.3g, of which saturates 18.5g; Cholesterol 342mg; Calcium 104mg; Fibre 0.5g; Sodium 375mg.

Venison tenderloins with cherry sauce
Dyrefilet med kirsebær sovs

Served mainly in autumn or winter during the hunting season, venison's rich flavour and earthy taste have led to a revival in its popularity. Creamed parsnips go well with this dish together with some braised leeks.

1 Preheat the oven to 230°C/450°F/Gas 8. Tie the venison at 2.5cm/1in intervals with fine string to hold its shape while roasting. Sprinkle with salt and pepper, and spread with butter. Place on a rack in a shallow roasting pan, and pour in the water. Cook in the hot oven for 20 minutes to brown the surface.

2 Lower the heat to 180°C/350°F/Gas 4. Continue to cook the tenderloin, basting at intervals with the pan juices, for a further 1¼ hours, until barely pink in the centre (65°C/150°F on a meat thermometer). Leave the meat in a warm place to rest for 10 minutes before slicing.

3 Meanwhile, to make the sauce, bring the cherry juice to the boil in a pan over a medium-high heat. Whisk together the water and cornflour in a small bowl, and stir into the cherry juice. Cook the sauce, stirring constantly, until the mixture thickens. Stir in the cherries and bring the mixture back to the boil. Serve with the venison.

Per portion Energy 518kcal/2197kJ; Protein 74.6g; Carbohydrate 37.5g, of which sugars 33.7g; Fat 10.8g, of which saturates 4.8g; Cholesterol 176mg; Calcium 45mg; Fibre 0.4g; Sodium 220mg.

Serves 4–6

2–2.5kg/4½–5½lb venison tenderloin

25g/1oz/2 tbsp butter, softened

250ml/8fl oz/1 cup water

salt and ground black pepper

For the cherry sauce

250ml/8fl oz/1 cup cherry juice

120ml/4fl oz/½ cup water

25ml/1½ tbsp cornflour (cornstarch)

425g/15oz canned or frozen unsweetened stoned (pitted) cherries

90g/3½oz/½ cup sugar, or to taste

salt

Serves 4

1 duck, about 1.8–2.5kg/4–5½lb, with giblets

150g/5oz stoned (pitted) prunes, sliced

2 medium dessert apples, peeled and chopped

20g/3/4oz fine breadcrumbs

475ml/16fl oz/2 cups chicken stock

small bay leaf

30ml/2 tbsp plain (all-purpose) flour

15ml/1 tbsp single (light) cream

salt and white pepper

Cook's tips
• When buying duck, allow at least 450g/1lb per person to accommodate the fat lost during cooking.
• If the duck is getting too brown during cooking, make a foil tent to shield it from the heat.
• Serve the duck with lingonberry or cherry sauce.
• Add a few sultanas to the prune stuffing mixture.

Roast duck with prunes and apples
Stegt and med svesker og æbler

Christmas Eve dinner in Denmark traditionally featured a plump roast goose stuffed with sliced apples and prunes – a bird that signalled a family's prosperity and wellbeing. In modern times, duck has replaced its larger cousin as the holiday bird. The same classic apple and prune stuffing works equally well. At Christmas, serve with roast potatoes, lingonberry sauce, and braised red cabbage; at other times serve more simply with steamed cauliflower.

1 Preheat the oven to 240°C/475°F/Gas 9. Rinse the duck and pat dry with kitchen paper. Score the breast with a crosshatch pattern. Season well.

2 Toss the prunes and apples with the breadcrumbs in a bowl and spoon this mixture into the duck cavity, packing it firmly. Close the opening with skewers or sew up with fine string.

3 Pour 250ml/8fl oz/1 cup of the chicken stock into a roasting pan. Place the duck on a rack in the roasting pan, breast side down, and cook for 20 minutes.

4 Put the giblets in a pan with 475ml/16fl oz/2 cups water and the bay leaf. Bring to a rolling boil for 20–30 minutes until reduced. Strain and set aside.

5 Lower the oven heat to 180°C/350°F/Gas 4. Remove the roasting pan from the oven and turn the duck breast side up. Pour the remaining stock into the pan. Continue to cook for 40 minutes per kg/20 minutes per lb, until the juices run clear when the thickest part of the leg is pierced. Transfer the duck to a serving dish and leave in a warm place to rest for 10 minutes before carving.

6 To make the gravy, pour off the fat from the roasting pan and whisk the flour into the remaining juices. Cook the mixture over a medium heat for 2–3 minutes until light brown. Gradually whisk in the giblet stock and stir in the cream. Cook the gravy, stirring, for 3 minutes more, pour into a sauceboat and serve with the duck.

Per portion Energy 663kcal/2757kJ; Protein 31.6g; Carbohydrate 24g, of which sugars 14.6g; Fat 49.6g, of which saturates 14g; Cholesterol 100mg; Calcium 55mg; Fibre 2.8g; Sodium 222mg.

Braised chicken
Gammeldags kylling

Braising is a favourite method of cooking chicken in Denmark. The simple method works especially well as a tenderizing technique for older hens. It's also adaptable for a whole bird or one cut into serving pieces. Once the chicken is browned, the dish can be cooked on top of the stove or in the oven. Serve the braised chicken with new potatoes and Cucumber salad to create another classic Danish meal.

1 Rinse the chicken and pat dry, inside and out, with kitchen paper. Rub the skin with lemon juice, salt and pepper.

2 Melt the butter in a heavy pan, which has a tight-fitting lid, over a medium heat. Add the chicken pieces and cook for about 15 minutes, turning, until they are browned all over.

3 Pour half the stock over the chicken, add the squeezed lemon half, and cover. Simmer, basting with the remaining stock, for 30 minutes.

4 Add the leeks and carrots to the chicken and cook for a further 30 minutes, or until the juices run clear when the chicken is pierced. Lift out the chicken and vegetables and keep them warm. Discard the lemon half.

5 Raise the heat, bring the stock to the boil, and reduce the liquid until you have a tasty, slightly thickened gravy. Add the cream and heat through until thick and smooth. Season to taste with salt and pepper and return the chicken and vegetables to the pan to warm through.

6 Serve the chicken with the vegetables and gravy together with some boiled new potatoes and a Cucumber salad.

Serves 4–6

1 roasting chicken, about 1.6–2kg/ 3½–4½lb, jointed

juice of ½ lemon

25g/1oz/2 tbsp butter

475ml/16fl oz/2 cups chicken stock

250g/9oz sliced leeks

6 small carrots, sliced lengthways,

175ml/6fl oz/¾ cup double (heavy) cream

salt and white pepper

Cook's tips

• This dish can also be prepared in the oven. Brown the chicken on the stove, then cover and place the pan in a preheated oven at 180°C/350°F/Gas 4. Cook for about 45 minutes, or until the juices run clear and add the vegetables half-way through the cooking time.

• For a modern variation use white wine instead of chicken stock.

Per portion Energy 8533kcal/35855kJ; Protein 343.7g; Carbohydrate 876.7g, of which sugars 621.4g; Fat 433.3g, of which saturates 17.8g; Cholesterol 211mg; Calcium 6538mg; Fibre 15.9g; Sodium 7641mg.

Serves 6–8

1 roasting chicken, about
1.6–2kg/3½–4½lb

½ lemon

60ml/4 tbsp chopped parsley

65g/2½oz/5 tbsp butter, softened

250ml/8fl oz/1 cup chicken stock or
water

350g/12oz/1½ cups unsweetened
lingonberries

100–150g/3¾–5oz/½–¾ cup caster
(superfine) sugar, to taste

salt and white pepper

Potato salad, to serve

Cook's tips

• Allow 40 minutes per kilogram/20
minutes per pound when oven-roasting
a chicken.

• Look for frozen, unsweetened
lingonberries in Scandinavian speciality
shops, or in the food market section at
IKEA, and sweeten to taste. A ready-
made lingonberry preserve could also
be used.

• The Danes do not include green
salads with their meals very often but a
green salad of mixed leaves dressed
with oil and vinegar would go very well
with this meal.

Roast chicken with lingonberries
Stegt kylling med tyttebærsovs

*Traditional Sunday dinner in Denmark often features sliced, roast chicken
served cold with potato salad, and a sauce of tart-sweet lingonberries or
cowberries, a meal that's easy on the cook. The berries, small cranberry-like
fruit, grow wild throughout Scandinavia's mountainous northern climes. Look for
frozen, unsweetened lingonberries, which are easy to sweeten to taste.*

1 Preheat the oven to 220°C/425°F/Gas 7. Rinse the chicken and pat dry inside
and out with kitchen paper. Rub with lemon and season with salt and pepper.

2 Mix together the parsley and 40g/1½oz/3 tbsp of the butter and spread this
inside the chicken. Close the opening with a skewer or fine string. Pour half the
chicken stock or water into a roasting pan and place the chicken, breast side up,
on a rack in the pan. Melt the remaining butter and brush half of it over the
chicken. Roast for 30 minutes.

3 Lower the oven temperature to 180°C/350°F/Gas 4. Pour the remaining stock or
water into the pan. Baste the chicken with the remaining melted butter and the pan
juices and continue to cook for a further 30–40 minutes, until the juices run clear
when the thickest part of the thigh is pierced. Remove from the oven, cover and
leave to cool. Refrigerate the cooled chicken until ready to slice for serving.

4 Place the lingonberries in a bowl. Add the sugar a little at a time, stirring until the
sugar thoroughly dissolves and the fruit is mashed. Add more sugar to taste and
chill the lingonberries until ready to serve.

5 Remove the chicken from the fridge half an hour before serving so that the meat
is not too chilled. Just before you are ready to eat, carve the chicken and arrange
the slices, together with the whole legs and wings on a serving platter. Serve with
Potato salad and the lingonberry sauce.

Per portion Energy 405kcal/1682kJ; Protein 24.9g; Carbohydrate 15.3g, of which sugars 15.3g; Fat
27.4g, of which saturates 10.2g; Cholesterol 145mg; Calcium 36mg; Fibre 1.4g; Sodium 151mg.

Desserts & baking

Red berry soup with cream

Cold buttermilk soup

Beer soup with whipped cream

Danish dried fruit soup

Old-fashioned apple cake

Lemon mousse

Rice pudding with warm cherry sauce

National Day dessert

Layer cake with cream and raspberries

Swiss roll

Danish-style doughnuts

Almond ring cake

Plum cake

Lenten buns with vanilla cream

Mazarins

Danish pastry

Vanilla rings

Dark rye bread

Seasonal sweets and buttery baked treats

The sign of a golden pretzel has identified a bakery or pastry shop in Denmark since medieval times. Beneath it, the window overflows with tantalizing pastries, marzipan, tartlets, meringues, biscuits, dense rye breads and much more. Danish bakers are famous for elevating buttery puff pastry to its highest form as *weinerbrød* (Vienna bread). It's often imitated, but Danish flour and cultured butter give Danish pastry its outstanding characteristics. Another original creation is the Almond ring cake, a festive tower of baked marzipan served at weddings and other important family events.

The custom of serving freshly baked treats to guests at home is deeply ingrained in Danish culture. Every cook has an extensive repertoire of cakes and biscuits to serve with coffee. Layer cakes and Swiss rolls are coffee table favourites, along with Plum cake and Mazarins, and no cook would be without at least seven different kinds of biscuit at Christmas.

Traditional desserts tend to be simple and seasonal, a legacy of the country's rural past. In spring, rhubarb is stirred into National Day dessert. Summer fruits are celebrated in a tangy-sweet soup, swirled with cream. Apples in autumn inspire Old-fashioned apple cake and in winter, dried fruit simmers with spices to make a warm dessert soup. Beer is the key ingredient in a very old, tasty peasant dessert made with cream, eggs, breadcrumbs and sugar.

For holidays, Lenten buns delight all ages at *Fastelavn* (Shrovetide). At Christmas, doughnut-like *æbleskiver* are served with warm, spiced red wine called *glögg*. Creamy rice pudding topped with a cherry sauce is the traditional dessert for Christmas Eve dinner.

Red berry soup with cream
Rødgrød med fløde

Some call this ruby-red berry soup Denmark's national dessert. Utterly simple to prepare, it can be made using a blend of various red berries. Currants and raspberries are the traditional combination, but raspberries and strawberries, red and blackcurrants, or currants and cherries are also delightful. Served cold with a swirl of cream in each bowl, the soup is sweet and tangy.

1 Put the berries, sugar and 500ml/17fl oz/generous 2 cups of the blackcurrant juice into a pan and add 750ml/1¼ pints/3 cups water. Bring the mixture to the boil and cook over a medium-high heat for 3 minutes. Pour the fruit and juice through a strainer set over a pan. Use a wooden spoon to press through as much berry juice as possible.

2 In a small bowl, mix the cornflour with the remaining blackcurrant juice. Stir the cornflour mixture into the berry juice. Place the pan over a medium heat and bring the juice to the boil, stirring, until it thickens slightly.

3 Pour the cream into a bowl and stir in the vanilla sugar. Pour the soup into individual bowls and spoon 30ml/2 tbsp cream into each bowl, swirling it slightly. Sprinkle each bowl with a few raspberries and serve.

Per portion Energy 383kcal/1606kJ; Protein 3.1g; Carbohydrate 44g, of which sugars 37.1g; Fat 23g, of which saturates 14.1g; Cholesterol 57mg; Calcium 84mg; Fibre 3.6g; Sodium 25mg.

Serves 6

400g/14oz redcurrants

450g/1lb raspberries

100–150g/3¾–5oz/½–¾ cup sugar (depending on the sweetness of the fruit)

550ml/18fl oz/2½ cups blackcurrant juice

45ml/3 tbsp cornflour (cornstarch)

250ml/8fl oz/1 cup double (heavy) cream

10ml/2 tsp vanilla sugar

raspberries, to decorate

Cook's tip Chopped, fresh rhubarb blended with berries can also be used to make this dessert. Potato flour can be substituted for cornflour, but do not boil the soup after adding it or it will become rubbery.

Serves 6

2 large eggs, separated

1.5ml/¼ tsp cream of tartar

130g/4½oz/⅔ cup caster
(superfine) sugar

5ml/1 tsp vanilla extract

2.5ml/½ tsp freshly grated
lemon zest

1.5 litres/2½ pints/6¼ cups buttermilk

50g/2oz/¼ cup flaked (sliced) almonds,
toasted, to decorate

Cook's tip Toast the almonds
under the grill (broiler) on a low heat.
Be careful not to burn them.

Note: Raw eggs are not
recommended for very young
children and pregnant women.

Cold buttermilk soup
Kærnemælks koldskål

*Light and frothy, with subtle sweetness and lemony notes, this refreshing cold
dessert soup is delightfully simple to prepare. Don't be put off by the buttermilk
base: it gives no sour taste to the soup, only a creamy richness. Always a
summer favourite, for many Danes this dish brings back fond childhood
memories: in many families kammerjunkere (tiny sugar cookies) were floated on
top of the soup – when they were called "little ducks". The toasted almonds
add a similar crunchy contrast to the smooth, cold soup.*

1 Beat the egg whites until frothy in a medium bowl, then add the cream of tartar.
Continue beating until stiff peaks form. Set aside.

2 In a second bowl, beat the egg yolks with the sugar. Add the vanilla extract and
lemon zest. Stir in the buttermilk and blend the mixture thoroughly.

3 Gently fold the egg whites into the buttermilk mixture, stirring to blend. Serve
immediately in soup plates or bowls, decorated with the toasted almonds.

Per portion Energy 241kcal/1017kJ; Protein 12.5g; Carbohydrate 34.2g, of which sugars 34g; Fat 7.3g,
of which saturates 1.2g; Cholesterol 73mg; Calcium 346mg; Fibre 0.6g; Sodium 136mg.

3 slices dark rye or pumpernickel bread

1 litre/1¾ pints/4 cups beer or medium dark ale

2 cinnamon sticks, approximately 7.5cm/3in long

45ml/3 tbsp caster (superfine) sugar

5ml/1 tsp vanilla sugar

½ lemon, cut into wedges

2 egg yolks

250ml/8fl oz/1 cup single (light) cream

350ml/12fl oz/1½ cups double (heavy) cream

salt

Beer soup with whipped cream
Øllebrød med flødeskum

One of the most intriguing dishes in the Danish recipe repertoire, this simple, soup combines beer, bread and cream with spices. It has been described as tasting like liquid gingerbread, and is considered an effective antidote to a hangover. The soup was traditionally served for breakfast as well as for special occasions. Hearty and simple, this soup is surprisingly delicious.

1 Toast the bread. Shred the toast into coarse crumbs and place in a pan. Pour the beer over the crumbs, and leave to soak for 15 minutes.

2 Add the cinnamon, sugar, vanilla sugar and lemon wedges, with a pinch of salt, to the beer mixture. Simmer the mixture, stirring occasionally, for about 15 minutes, then remove and discard the lemon wedges.

3 Meanwhile, slowly beat the egg yolks in a mixing bowl with the single cream and 250ml/8fl oz/1 cup of the double cream until well blended. Stir in a ladleful of the hot beer mixture to temper the eggs. Remove the beer mixture from the heat and slowly stir into the egg mixture.

4 Beat the remaining double cream until soft peaks form. When ready to serve the soup, spoon a dollop of cream into each bowl.

Per portion Energy 517kcal/2144kJ; Protein 5.8g; Carbohydrate 25.7g, of which sugars 20.2g; Fat 35.6g, of which saturates 21.6g; Cholesterol 156mg; Calcium 118mg; Fibre 0.6g; Sodium 127mg.

Danish dried fruit soup
Varm frugtsuppe

Throughout Scandinavia, soups made with dried fruit used to be especially welcome during the long, dark winter months when fresh fruit was unavailable. Any combination of dried fruit can be used; pears and peaches are a modern addition, but faithful to the soup's heritage.

1 Chop all the dried fruit and place in a large pan together with 1 litre/1¾ pints/4 cups water. Cover, and leave to stand for at least 2 hours or overnight.

2 Stir the lemon zest, cinnamon stick, cloves and tapioca into the dried fruit mixture. Bring to the boil, cover and simmer gently for 1 hour, stirring occasionally.

3 Remove the pan from the heat. Remove the cinnamon stick and discard. Let the fruit mixture cool slightly.

4 Beat the double cream until soft peaks form. Serve the warm fruit soup with a dollop of cream in each bowl.

Per portion Energy 305kcal/1277kJ; Protein 2.7g; Carbohydrate 37.4g, of which sugars 31.5g; Fat 17.1g, of which saturates 10.4g; Cholesterol 43mg; Calcium 51mg; Fibre 4g; Sodium 17mg.

Serves 6–8

50g/2oz/¼ cup currants

50g/2oz/¼ cup sultanas (golden raisins)

115g/4oz/½ cup dried apricots

115g/4oz/½ cup prunes

115g/4oz/½ cup dried apples

115g/4oz/½ cup dried peaches

115g/4oz/½ cup dried pears

15ml/1 tbsp lemon zest

7.5cm/3in cinnamon stick

5 whole cloves

40g/1½oz/¼ cup quick-cook tapioca

250ml/8fl oz/1 cup double (heavy) cream

Old-fashioned apple cake
Gammeldags æblekage

This cake has another lovely name in Danish: it's called Bondepige med Slør, *which means 'peasant girl in a veil'. It is traditionally served on St Martin's Day, 11 November. In fact, this old-fashioned dessert is not really a cake at all, but an easy-to-make layered confection of sweetened breadcrumbs, stewed apples and whipped cream. Use a glass bowl to show the different layers, and assemble about an hour before serving so the breadcrumbs stay crisp.*

1 Peel and core the apples and cut them into chunks. Place them in a heavy pan with 250ml/8fl oz/1 cup of water, the sugar, cinnamon, nutmeg and cloves (if using). Cover and cook over a low heat, stirring occasionally, for about 25 minutes, until soft but still chunky. Remove from the heat and leave to cool.

2 Melt the butter in a frying pan. Stir in the breadcrumbs and brown sugar, tossing to coat the crumbs evenly with the butter. Cook, stirring, for about 4 minutes until the crumbs are lightly browned and toasted. Remove from the heat and set aside.

3 Beat the double cream until soft peaks form and stir in the icing and vanilla sugars. Place a thin layer of breadcrumbs in the bottom of six serving glasses or bowls, cover the breadcrumbs with a layer of apple, then a layer of cream. Repeat the layers, ending with cream. Chill, then decorate before serving.

Per portion Energy 498kcal/2090kJ; Protein 4.7g; Carbohydrate 64.3g, of which sugars 42.5g; Fat 26.5g, of which saturates 16.1g; Cholesterol 66mg; Calcium 79mg; Fibre 3.3g; Sodium 261mg.

Serves 6

1kg/2¼lb tart eating apples

90g/3½oz/½ cup sugar, or to taste

5ml/1 tsp cinnamon

1.5ml/¼ tsp nutmeg

1.5ml/¼ tsp ground cloves (optional)

25g/1oz/2 tbsp butter

175g/6oz/3 cups fresh breadcrumbs

25g/1oz/2 tbsp soft brown sugar

250ml/8fl oz/1 cup double (heavy) cream

10ml/2 tsp icing (confectioners') sugar

5ml/1 tsp vanilla sugar

chopped nuts or grated chocolate, to decorate

Serves 6–8

50ml/2fl oz/¼ cup apple juice or water

30ml/2 tbsp powdered gelatine

15ml/1 tbsp grated lemon zest

90ml/6 tbsp fresh lemon juice

4 eggs, separated

175g/6oz icing (confectioner's) sugar

250ml/8fl oz/1 cup double (heavy) cream

Note: Raw eggs are not recommended for very young children and pregnant women.

Cook's tips Crumble macaroons into the bottom of dessert glasses and spoon the mousse over them.

Lemon mousse
Citronfromage

Light and airy, this heavenly dessert is also easy to make and refreshing. Its Danish name alludes to the influence of French culinary traditions in the 1800s.

1 Pour the apple juice or water into a small bowl. Add the gelatine until softened. Add 120ml/4fl oz/½ cup boiling water and stir to dissolve the gelatine, then stir in the lemon zest and juice.

2 Combine the egg yolks with 150g/5oz/1¼ cups of the icing sugar in a bowl, and beat until frothy. Fold the gelatine mixture into the egg yolks. Refrigerate for at least 1 hour. Beat the egg whites until stiff and fold them into the egg yolk mixture.

3 Beat the cream until stiff peaks form, and stir in the remaining icing sugar. Fold half the cream into the egg and lemon mixture.

4 Spoon the mousse into a deep, 2 litre/3½ pint glass bowl or 6 individual bowls. Chill until set. Serve decorated with the remaining whipped cream and lemon zest.

Per portion Energy 278kcal/1159kJ; Protein 3.7g; Carbohydrate 23.4g, of which sugars 23.4g; Fat 19.6g, of which saturates 11.2g; Cholesterol 138mg; Calcium 41mg; Fibre 0g; Sodium 43mg.

Serves 6–8

1.5 litres/2½ pints/6¼ cups milk

1 vanilla pod (bean)

225g/8oz/1 cup short grain rice

25g/1oz/2 tbsp caster (superfine) sugar

25g/1oz/2 tbsp vanilla sugar

50g/2oz/1/2 cup chopped blanched almonds

1 whole almond

250ml/8fl oz/1 cup double (heavy) cream

For the cherry sauce

450g/1lb fresh or bottled dark cherries, stoned (pitted), cut into quarters

90g/3½ oz/½ cup sugar

5ml/1 tsp fresh lemon juice

2 whole cloves

30ml/2 tbsp cornflour (cornstarch)

Rice pudding with warm cherry sauce
Ris á l'amande med varm kirsebær sovs

At Christmas time this pudding comes with a surprise: whoever finds a whole almond in their serving wins a prize, usually a plump little marzipan pig.

1 Pour the milk into the top of a double boiler. Slit open the vanilla pod and scrape the seeds into the milk; add the pod. Bring the milk to the boil. Add the rice to the boiling milk, lower the heat, cover, and cook for 2 hours, stirring occasionally, until almost all the milk is absorbed. Remove the lid for the last 10 minutes.

2 Remove the rice mixture from the heat and leave to cool slightly. While it is still warm, stir in the caster sugar, vanilla sugar, chopped almonds and whole almond. Chill the pudding. Whip the cream until stiff and gently fold it into the cold rice pudding. Turn into a serving dish and chill until ready to serve.

3 To make the sauce, put the cherries in a pan with 475ml/16fl oz/2 cups water, the sugar, lemon juice and cloves. Bring to the boil and cook gently, stirring, for about 20 minutes. Transfer a small amount of the cherry juice to a small bowl. Add the cornflour to the juice and blend to a smooth paste. Stir the cornflour mixture into the cherries and cook for 10 minutes more, until thickened. Remove from the heat and cool. Serve drizzled over the rice pudding.

Per portion Energy 503kcal/2107kJ; Protein 10.7g; Carbohydrate 64.4g, of which sugars 38.3g; Fat 23.6g, of which saturates 12.7g; Cholesterol 54mg; Calcium 279mg; Fibre 0.8g; Sodium 96mg.

National Day dessert
Grundlovsdessert

This frothy pink pudding celebrates Denmark's National Day, commemorating the change from a constitutional monarchy to a parliamentary democracy when Frederick IX signed the new Constitution on 5 June 1953.

1 Cut the rhubarb into 2.5cm/1in pieces and place in a pan. Add half the sugar, the lemon juice and 250ml/8fl oz/1 cup water. Bring to the boil, then reduce the heat and simmer gently for 15 minutes until the rhubarb is soft.

2 Pour the milk into a pan. Slit open the vanilla pod and scrape the seeds into the milk; add the vanilla pod. Bring the milk to the boil, reduce the heat and simmer for 2 minutes. Remove from the heat to cool, and discard the vanilla pod. Soften the gelatine in 30ml/2 tbsp cold water, then pour on 120ml/4fl oz/½ cup boiling water and stir until dissolved.

3 Combine the egg yolks with the remaining sugar in a mixing bowl, and beat until light and thick. Stir the gelatine mixture into the egg yolks with the vanilla-flavoured milk and leave to thicken. Beat the egg whites into stiff peaks and fold gently into the thickened egg yolk and milk mixture. Add a drop of red food colouring and blend until the pudding is coloured pale pink.

4 Beat the cream until stiff, fold half into the egg mixture. Divide the rhubarb among six bowls and spoon over the pudding. Top with a spoonful of whipped cream and sprinkle with almonds. Chill until ready to serve.

Per portion Energy 375kcal/1566kJ; Protein 11.6g; Carbohydrate 23.6g, of which sugars 23.6g; Fat 26.9g, of which saturates 15.4g; Cholesterol 186mg; Calcium 204mg; Fibre 1.6g; Sodium 78mg.

Serves 6

675g/1½lb rhubarb

115g/4oz/½ cup caster (superfine) sugar

30ml/2 tbsp fresh lemon juice

250ml/8fl oz/1 cup milk

1 vanilla pod (bean)

30ml/2 tbsp powdered gelatine

4 eggs, separated

1 drop red food colouring

250ml/8fl oz/1 cup double (heavy) cream

flaked (sliced) almonds, to decorate

Cook's tip Crumble almond macaroons in the bottom of the bowls before adding the rhubarb.

Serves 10–12

For the cake

115g/4oz/½ cup unsalted (sweet) butter

200g/7oz/1 cup caster (superfine) sugar

4 eggs, separated

45ml/3 tbsp milk

175g/6oz/1½ cups plain (all-purpose) flour

25ml/1½ tbsp cornflour (cornstarch)

7.5ml/1½ tsp baking powder

1.5ml/¼ tsp salt

5ml/1 tsp vanilla sugar

fresh raspberries, to decorate

For the raspberry filling

375g/13oz/3 cups raspberries, crushed in a bowl, with sugar to taste

For the custard filling

2 eggs

90g/3½ oz/½ cup caster (superfine) sugar

15ml/1 tbsp potato flour or cornflour

350ml/12fl oz/1½ cups milk

pinch of salt

For the cream topping

475ml/16fl oz/2 cups double (heavy) cream or whipping cream

25g/1oz/¼ cup icing (confectioners') sugar

5ml/1 tsp vanilla sugar

Layer cake with cream and raspberries
Lagkage med fløderskum og hindbær

Fondly known as the Danish birthday cake, this lovely, traditional cake is popular all over Scandinavia in slightly varying forms. For birthday celebrations, it is decorated with Danish flags and candles. For the best flavour, bake the cake a day before assembling the layers.

1 Lightly grease and flour three 23cm/9in layer cake tins (pans). Preheat the oven to 230°C/450°F/Gas 8. Cream the butter with the sugar in a mixing bowl until light and fluffy. Beat in the egg yolks, one at a time. Stir in the milk until blended.

2 In a separate bowl, sift together the flour, cornflour, baking powder, salt and vanilla sugar. Fold the flour mixture into the egg mixture until smooth.

3 Beat the eggs whites in a separate bowl until stiff peaks form. Gently fold the egg whites into the cake mixture. Divide evenly among the three tins and smooth to the edges of the tins. Bake in the hot oven for 12 minutes. Leave the cakes to cool for 10 minutes, then remove from the tins and cool on a rack.

4 To make the custard, whisk together the eggs and sugar in a pan until well blended. Whisk in the potato flour or cornflour and milk. Add the salt. Cook over a low heat, stirring, for about 6 minutes. Remove from the heat and leave to cool.

5 Beat the cream in a bowl until soft peaks form. Stir in the icing sugar and vanilla sugar; continue beating until stiff.

6 To assemble the cake, invert one layer on a serving plate and spread with raspberry filling. Place a second cake layer over the first and spread it with the cooled custard. Top with the final layer. Spread whipped cream over the sides and top of the cake. Chill the cake until ready to serve, and decorate with raspberries.

Per portion Energy 433kcal/1811kJ; Protein 6.1g; Carbohydrate 44.6g, of which sugars 30.4g; Fat 27g, of which saturates 15.9g; Cholesterol 157mg; Calcium 86mg; Fibre 1.2g; Sodium 109mg.

Serves 12

50g/2oz/½ cup self-raising (self-rising) flour

25g/1oz/¼ cup potato flour or cornflour

5ml/1 tsp baking powder

3 eggs

250g/9oz/1¼ cups caster (superfine) sugar

30ml/2 tbsp water

For the chocolate buttercream filling

50g/2oz/¼ cup unsalted (sweet) butter

90g/3oz/⅔ cup icing (confectioner's) sugar, sifted

1 egg yolk

30ml/2tbsp unsweetened cocoa powder, sifted, plus extra for dusting

Swiss roll
Roulade

Rolled sponge cakes are frequently served for dessert in Denmark, accompanied by strong black coffee. They are easy to make and versatile, with delectable fillings that range from fresh fruit to buttercream.

1 Preheat the oven to 190°C/375°F/Gas 5. Lightly grease a 27 x 38cm/10½ x 15in Swiss roll tin (jelly roll pan). Line with baking parchment and lightly grease.

2 Sift together the flour, potato flour and baking powder in a mixing bowl. Whisk the eggs and 150g/5oz/¾ cup of the sugar together in a separate bowl until light and foamy. Gradually fold the flour into the egg mixture, continuing to beat until smooth. Add the water. Spread the batter evenly over the prepared tin and bake for 10–12 minutes until golden brown. Sprinkle a clean dish towel with the remaining sugar.

3 To make the chocolate buttercream filling, cream the butter and icing sugar until light and fluffy. Stir in the egg yolk until well blended, add the cocoa and blend.

4 Turn the cooked cake out on to the prepared towel, remove the parchment, and trim the edges. While warm, roll the cake up with the towel inside and set aside. When the cake is cool, unroll it, spread with buttercream and roll up again, without the towel. Place the cake on a serving plate with the seam facing down and serve.

Per portion Energy 196kcal/826kJ; Protein 2.8g; Carbohydrate 35.1g, of which sugars 29.7g; Fat 5.9g, of which saturates 3g; Cholesterol 73mg; Calcium 34mg; Fibre 0.4g; Sodium 70mg.

Danish-style doughnuts
Æbleskiver

These plump, round doughy balls, warm and crisp on the outside and soft in the middle, date from the 1600s, and are cooked in a special cast iron griddle.

1 Heat the milk to tepid and dissolve the yeast in it. Set aside. Cream the butter with the sugar in a mixing bowl until light. Beat in the egg yolks and stir in the cream. In a separate bowl, combine the flour, bicarbonate of soda, salt, lemon rind and cardamom. Stir the flour mixture into the egg yolk mixture, alternating with the yeast mixture, until well blended.

2 Beat the egg whites in a separate bowl until stiff peaks form. Gently fold into the flour mixture. Cover the bowl, and leave the batter to rest for 1 hour.

3 Heat the griddle over a low to medium heat. Test the temperature by sprinkling a few drops of water: if it jumps and sputters, the pan is ready. Add 10ml/2 tsp cooking oil into each cup. Pour batter into each cup, to within 3mm/⅛in of the top. Cook until the bottom is set and golden. Use a metal knitting needle to rotate the ball a one-quarter turn. Repeat until the balls are golden brown all over. Take care not to pierce the balls when turning them.

4 Pile the *æbleskiver* balls on a plate and dust with icing sugar while still warm. Serve with spoonfuls of apple jelly, or drizzle with lingonberry jam.

Per portion Energy 118kcal/489kJ; Protein 1.8g; Carbohydrate 7.2g, of which sugars 1.5g; Fat 9.3g, of which saturates 2.6g; Cholesterol 27mg; Calcium 30mg; Fibre 0.2g; Sodium 23mg.

Makes 24–30

250ml/8fl oz/1 cup milk

15g/½oz fresh yeast

50g/2oz/¼ cup unsalted (sweet) butter

25g/1oz/2 tbsp caster (superfine) sugar

3 eggs, separated

200ml/7fl oz/scant 1 cup single (light) cream

225g/8oz/2 cups plain (all-purpose) flour, sifted

5ml/1 tsp bicarbonate of soda (baking soda)

1.5ml/¼ tsp salt

10ml/2 tsp grated lemon rind

5ml/1 tsp ground cardamom

250ml/8fl oz/1 cup cooking oil

raspberry jam or apple jelly, and icing (confectioners') sugar to serve

Serves 24

For the cake

250g/9oz/2½ cups blanched almonds, finely ground

250g/9oz/2½ cups almonds with skins on, finely ground

500g/1¼lb/4½ cups icing (confectioners') sugar, sifted

3 egg whites

For the icing

1 egg white

175g/6oz/1½ cups icing (confectioners') sugar, sifted

pinch of salt

5ml/1 tsp double (heavy) cream

Cook's tips
• To enhance the almond flavour, lightly toast the blanched almonds in the oven at 160°C/325°F/Gas 3 for 10 minutes, turning once, before grinding them.
• The dough will be very stiff, but it can be spooned into a piping (pastry) bag fitted with a wide, round tip, and piped into the tins.

Almond ring cake
Kransekage

Unique to the baking traditions of Denmark and Norway, towers assembled from stacked rings of marzipan cake are served at festive occasions, and at special "round" birthdays at the start of a new decade. Special sets of ring cake tins, 15 or 18 to a set, are often used to make the cake, but if these aren't available, the dough can be rolled by hand and looped round into rings.

1 Preheat the oven to 200°C/400°F/Gas 6. If using *kransekage* tins (pans), grease 16–18 tins. (Non-stick tins also work best when greased.)

2 To make the cake, combine all the ground almonds with the sugar in a large pan. Add the unbeaten egg white and mix into a firm dough. Place the pan over a low heat and knead until the dough is almost too hot to handle.

3 Roll out the dough into sausages about 1cm/½in in diameter and fit them into the prepared tins. Press the overlapping ends together to make a smooth circle. If you are not using tins, line two baking sheets with baking parchment. Draw a 17cm/6½in diameter circle on the paper. Draw circles in decreasing sizes, each 1 cm/½ in smaller than the last, ending with a 5cm/2in circle. Roll the dough into sausages and fit one into each circle, piecing them together as necessary. Bake the rings in the preheated oven for about 8 minutes, until the tops are a light golden brown. Remove from the oven and leave to cool in the tins.

4 To make the icing, beat the egg white until stiff, then stir in the icing sugar with the salt. Continue beating until the mixture is soft. Stir in the cream, and beat for 1 minute. Pour the icing into a piping (pastry) bag fitted with a 1.5mm/¹⁄₁₆in nozzle.

5 To assemble the cake, place the largest ring on a serving plate. Stack the remaining rings on top of one another with the smallest on top, adding a covering of icing each time, piped on in a swirling, looping pattern. Finish with a final swirl of icing, and then decorate the cake with little Danish flags.

Per portion Energy 241kcal/1013kJ; Protein 5g; Carbohydrate 30.8g, of which sugars 30.3g; Fat 11.7g, of which saturates 1g; Cholesterol 0mg; Calcium 65mg; Fibre 1.5g; Sodium 15mg.

Plum cake
Blommerkage

Seasonal cooking is an obvious necessity in countries of the far north with fierce extremes of climate. Traditionally, you ate what you could grow and stored food carefully to survive until the next harvest. Fruit trees were especially prized and apple, pear and plum trees still thrive in many areas of Scandinavia. These fruits are treasured in traditional Danish cooking, adding sweetness, texture and variety to many dishes. This cardamom-accented cake has an intriguing pale bluish-green hue from the plum skins.

1 Place the chopped plums in a pan and add the water. Bring to the boil over a medium heat and cook for 10–15 minutes, until soft. Set aside to cool. You will need 350ml/12fl oz/1½ cups stewed plums for the cake.

2 Preheat the oven to 180°C/350°F/Gas 4. Grease and flour a 24cm/9½ in springform cake tin (pan). Cream the butter with the sugar in a mixing bowl until light and fluffy. Beat in the eggs, one at a time. Stir in the stewed plums and the almonds. Add the baking soda, baking powder, cardamom and salt and stir until blended. Gradually stir in the flour, a few spoons at a time, and mix until blended.

3 Pour the mixture into the prepared tin. Place 15 plum halves around the circumference of the cake and the remaining three halves in the centre, cut sides down. Sprinkle the pearl sugar over the cake. Bake for 1 hour, or until the top springs back when lightly touched. Cool in the tin for 15 minutes before unfastening the ring.

4 Beat the double cream until soft peaks form. Stir in the vanilla sugar and the icing sugar and beat until thick. Serve the cake, still slightly warm, or at room temperature, in slices topped with a dollop of whipped cream.

Serves 10

450g/1lb stoned (pitted) fresh plums, coarsely chopped, plus 9 extra plums, stoned and halved, to decorate

300ml/½pint/1¼ cups water

115g/4oz/½ cup unsalted (sweet) butter, softened

200g/7oz/1 cup caster (superfine) sugar

3 eggs

90g/3½oz/¾ cup toasted, finely chopped almonds

5ml/1 tsp bicarbonate of soda (baking soda)

7.5ml/1½ tsp baking powder

5ml/1 tsp ground cardamom

1.5ml/¼ tsp salt

250g/9oz/2¼ cups plain (all-purpose) flour

15ml/1 tbsp pearl sugar, to decorate

250ml/8fl oz/1 cup double (heavy) cream

10ml/2 tsp vanilla sugar

10ml/2 tsp icing (confectioners') sugar

Cook's tip Scandinavian pearl sugar, large crystals with a pearly sheen, is used to decorate pastries, buns and cakes. If you can't find it, use coarsely crushed white sugar cubes.

Per portion Energy 311kcal/1308kJ; Protein 6.4g; Carbohydrate 44.5g, of which sugars 15.9g; Fat 13.2g, of which saturates 7.4g; Cholesterol 89mg; Calcium 86mg; Fibre 2.4g; Sodium 102mg.

Makes 24 buns

For the buns

50ml/2fl oz/¼ cup tepid water

40g/1½oz fresh yeast

175g/6oz/¾ cup unsalted (sweet) butter, softened

50g/2oz/¼ cup caster (superfine) sugar

2 eggs, plus 1 extra yolk

175ml/6fl oz/¾ cup milk

2.5ml/½ tsp salt

5ml/1 tsp ground cardamom

400g/14oz/3½ cups bread flour

For the filling

3 egg yolks

45ml/3 tbsp caster (superfine) sugar

10ml/2 tsp vanilla sugar

15ml/1 tbsp potato flour or cornflour (cornstarch)

475ml/16fl oz/2 cups milk

pinch of salt

For the icing

1 egg white

150g/5oz/1¼ cups icing (confectioner's) sugar, sifted

25g/1oz/¼ cup unsweetened cocoa powder, sifted

pinch of salt

5ml/1 tsp double (heavy) cream

30ml/2 tbsp pearl sugar, to decorate

Lenten buns with vanilla cream
Fastelavnsboller

Though very few Danes still observe the Lenten fast, the holiday survives as a festive, carnival-like occasion. Traditional treats include these plump, yeasty buns, with a cream filling and various toppings.

1 Pour the tepid water into a bowl and stir in the yeast until dissolved. Combine the butter and sugar in a mixing bowl and beat until light and fluffy. Beat in one whole egg and the extra yolk.

2 Briefly warm the milk in a pan over a low heat, add the yeast mixture and stir into the creamed butter mixture. Add the salt and cardamom. Stir in the flour, a little at a time, and mix to a soft dough, adding more flour if necessary.

3 Turn the dough out on to a lightly floured surface and knead for 5–7 minutes, until smooth and satiny. Lightly oil a large bowl. Place the dough in the bowl, cover with a towel, and leave in a warm place until doubled in size, about 1 hour.

4 To make the filling, whisk together the egg yolks and sugar in a pan until well blended. Whisk in the vanilla sugar, potato flour or cornflour and milk. Add the salt. Cook over a low heat, stirring constantly, for about 6 minutes, until the mixture thickens. Remove from the heat and leave to cool.

5 Lightly grease two baking sheets. Turn the dough out on to a lightly floured surface and divide into four. Cut each part into six equal pieces and shape into balls. Place on the prepared baking sheets. Make a 2cm/¾in diameter well in the centre of each roll, and fill with a spoonful of the cream filling. Cover with clear film (plastic wrap) and leave in a warm place for 1½–2 hours.

6 Preheat the oven to 220°C/425°F/Gas 7. Lightly beat the remaining egg and brush it over the buns. Bake for 12–15 minutes, until golden. Cool on a wire rack.

7 To make the icing, beat the egg white until stiff. Stir in the icing sugar, cocoa and salt and beat until the mixture is soft. Stir in the cream and beat for 1 minute. Spread the icing over the tops of the buns and sprinkle with pearl sugar.

Per portion Energy 186kcal/782kJ; Protein 3.9g; Carbohydrate 25.6g, of which sugars 12.2g; Fat 8.3g, of which saturates 4.6g; Cholesterol 67mg; Calcium 70mg; Fibre 0.6g; Sodium 77mg.

Mazarins
Mazariner

Inside a Danish bakery or konditori *the array of baked goods is astonishing. Influenced by 18th-century French, German and Austrian traditions, Danish pastry chefs created their own vast repertoire of baked goods, still beloved by contemporary Danes, including buttery little cakes, tartlets with jam, marzipan or custard fillings, puff pastries with chocolate and vanilla icing, and dozens of chocolate or almond flavoured biscuits. These tartlets are miniature Danish versions of a mazarin cake: a crisp pastry shell with an almond paste filling.*

1 To make the pastry, sift the flour and icing sugar into bowl, then rub in butter until the mixture resembles breadcrumbs. Stir in the egg yolk and use your fingers to work the mixture into a soft, smooth dough. Gather the dough into a ball, wrap in baking parchment and refrigerate for 1 hour.

2 Roll out the dough to a thickness of 3mm/⅛ in and use to line 12 oval-shaped, fluted tartlet tins. Place the tins on a baking sheet and refrigerate while you make the filling. Preheat the oven to 190°C/375°F/Gas 5.

3 To make the filling, cream the butter and sugar until light and fluffy. Add the beaten eggs, a little at a time, stirring vigorously to mix.

4 Stir the almonds into the mixture, and add the green food colouring (if using). Spoon the almond filling into the prepared pastry cases. Bake for about 20 minutes, until the tops are light brown. Cool on a rack.

5 To make the icing, break up the chocolate and melt it with the butter in a pan over a low heat. Cool slightly, then spread over the cooled mazarins.

Makes 12

For the pastry

150g/5oz/1¼ cups plain (all-purpose) flour

25g/1oz/¼ cup icing (confectioners') sugar

90g/3½ oz/7 tbsp unsalted butter

1 egg yolk

For the filling

65g/2½oz/5tbsp unsalted (sweet) butter

75g/3oz/⅔ cup icing (confectioners') sugar

2 small eggs, beaten

115g/4oz/1 cup ground blanched almonds

1 tiny drop green food colouring (optional)

For the icing

200g/7oz plain (semisweet) chocolate

25g/1oz/2 tbsp unsalted (sweet) butter

Cook's tip Dust the tops of the mazarins with sifted icing (confectioners') sugar, or make a plain icing using 115g/4oz/1 cup icing sugar mixed with 10ml/2 tsp warm water and 2.5ml/½ tsp almond extract.

Per portion Energy 347kcal/1446kJ; Protein 5.3g; Carbohydrate 29.8g, of which sugars 19.8g; Fat 23.8g, of which saturates 11.4g; Cholesterol 78mg; Calcium 59mg; Fibre 1.5g; Sodium 105mg.

Makes 2 pastry braids or 16 pastries

For the pastry

40g/1½oz fresh yeast

150ml/¼ pint/⅔ cup milk

120ml/4fl oz/½ cup double (heavy) cream

50g/2oz/¼ cup caster (superfine) sugar

2 eggs

5ml/1 tsp ground cardamom

5ml/1 tsp salt

5ml/1 tsp vanilla sugar

400g/14oz/3½ cups white bread flour

340g/12oz/1½ cups unsalted (sweet) butter, chilled

For the almond filling

115g/4oz/½ cup unsalted (sweet) butter

90g/3½oz/½ cup caster (superfine) sugar

50g/2oz/½ cup ground almonds

45ml/3 tbsp double (heavy) cream

2.5ml/½ tsp almond extract

75g/2½ oz/½ cup sultanas (golden raisins)

For the glaze

1 egg

30ml/2 tbsp milk

flaked (sliced) almonds, to decorate

Danish pastry
Weinerbrød

Buttery, flaky Danish pastry is unrivalled in the baking universe, and classic puff pastry is key to this delectable treat. Use the highest quality butter you can find, and keep the pastry as cold as you can while you are making it.

1 Dissolve the yeast in the milk in a small bowl. Heat the cream gently in a pan to barely lukewarm, 40°C/104°F. Stir the yeast mixture into the cream and leave to stand for 5 minutes.

2 Beat the sugar with the eggs in a large mixing bowl until light and frothy. Stir in the cardamom, salt and vanilla sugar. Add the yeast mixture and blend well. Gradually stir in the bread flour to make a soft dough. Knead the dough in the bowl for 2–3 minutes. Cover and refrigerate for at least 1 hour (or up to 8 hours).

3 Turn the chilled dough out on to a lightly floured surface. Dust a rolling pin with a little flour, and roll the dough out to a 40cm/16in square about 1cm/½in thick. Cut the butter into thin slices and place these side by side down the middle of the pastry square, ending about 2.5cm/1in from the edge of the dough. Fold over one side of the pastry to cover the butter, then the other side. Seal the ends. Wrap the dough with clear film (plastic wrap) and refrigerate for 15 minutes.

4 Unwrap the dough and roll out again to form a 40cm/16in square. Give the dough a quarter turn, then fold in thirds again, at right angles to the first folds. Wrap and refrigerate for another 15 minutes. Repeat the rolling, folding and chilling steps twice more, then cover and leave to rest in the fridge for 15 minutes.

5 Meanwhile, preheat the oven to 200°C/400°F/Gas 6. Prepare the filling by combining the butter, sugar and almonds in a bowl. Stir in the cream, almond extract and sultanas. Set aside. Line a baking sheet with baking parchment.

6 To make two Danish plaits, roll the dough out on a lightly floured surface to a 40cm/16in square. Cut the square into two rectangles and place them on the prepared baking sheet. Spread the prepared almond filling down the centre of each piece. Make diagonal cuts about 2cm/¾in apart down each side. Alternating sides, fold the strips in a criss-cross pattern over the filling in the centre.

7 For individual pastries, roll out the dough and cut into 10cm/4in squares. Spoon about 15ml/1tbsp of the filling into the centre of each square. Bake as a square, or fold opposite corners over to partially cover the filling. Repeat for each square, and place on prepared baking sheet.

8 Cover with a clean towel and leave for 15–30 minutes for the pastry to rise slightly. Combine the egg and milk in a small bowl and brush over the pastry. Sprinkle with flaked almonds and bake for about 15 minutes, until golden brown.

Per portion Energy 436kcal/1814kJ; Protein 5.1g; Carbohydrate 32.8g, of which sugars 13.7g; Fat 32.5g, of which saturates 18.9g; Cholesterol 111mg; Calcium 78mg; Fibre 1.1g; Sodium 194mg.

Makes 72

400g/14oz/1¾ cup butter
130g/4½oz/⅔ cup caster (superfine) sugar
1 egg
1 vanilla pod (bean), finely chopped, or 10ml/2 tsp vanilla extract
450g/1lb/4 cups plain (all-purpose) flour
1.5ml/¼ tsp bakers' ammonia (see Cook's Tip)
115g/4oz/1 cup blanched almonds, finely chopped

Cook's tip Bakers' ammonia (bicarbonate of ammonia) is used by Northern European cooks to make biscuits light and crisp. An ancestor of modern baking powder, it is also known as salt of hartshorn because it was originally obtained from ground reindeer antlers. Look for it in German or Scandinavian markets, pharmacies and baking supply stores. As a substitute, use 5ml/1 tsp baking powder, or 2.5ml/½ tsp baking powder with 2.5ml/½ tsp bicarbonate of soda (baking soda), but note that the biscuits will not be as light or crisp.

Vanilla rings
Vanillekranse

Danish baking is legendary the world around. Blessed with fine ingredients – butter, eggs and flour – from the country's prosperous farms, Danish pastry chefs and home cooks are renowned for creating artistically shaped and richly flavoured biscuits and cookies. For special occasions, family gatherings and Christmas festivities, no Danish table would be complete without an assortment of biscuits. These rich, buttery rings are a special favourite at Christmas.

1 Preheat the oven to 180°C/350°F/Gas 4. Lightly grease two baking sheets.

2 Place the butter and sugar in a large bowl and beat until light and fluffy. Beat in the egg, then the chopped vanilla pod or vanilla extract.

3 Gradually stir the flour, baker's ammonia and almonds into the creamed mixture to form a soft dough. Turn out on to a lightly floured surface and knead lightly until the dough is smooth.

4 Using a star piping nozzle or cookie press, form 5cm/2in diameter rings on the prepared baking sheets. Bake the biscuits for 8–9 minutes, until golden brown. Cool on a wire rack and store in an airtight container.

Per portion Energy 78kcal/326kJ; Protein 1g; Carbohydrate 6.3g, of which sugars 2.1g; Fat 5.6g, of which saturates 3g; Cholesterol 14mg; Calcium 14mg; Fibre 0.3g; Sodium 35mg.

Dark rye bread
Rugbrød

The Danish love affair with rye bread, whether light, dark, wholemeal or crispbread, is legendary. It's the thing Danes miss most when they leave home.

1 Dissolve the yeast in 250ml/8fl oz/1 cup warm water. Heat the buttermilk briefly in a pan over a low heat to barely lukewarm, 40°C/105°F. Stir the yeast mixture into the buttermilk and leave to stand for 5 minutes.

2 Add the butter and treacle to 250ml/8fl oz/1 cup boiling water and stir until the butter melts. Place the rye flour in a large mixing bowl and stir the butter mixture into the flour. Add the yeast mixture. Stir in the caraway seeds and salt. Gradually stir in the bread flour to make a soft, stiff dough. Knead the dough lightly in the bowl for 2–3 minutes.

3 Lightly butter a large bowl and place the dough in it. Cover the bowl and leave in a warm place for about 45 minutes until the dough has doubled in size. Preheat the oven to 200°C/400°F/Gas 6.

4 Lightly grease two 23 x 13cm/9 x 5in loaf tins (pans). Turn the dough out on to a lightly floured surface and knead again lightly. Form into two loaves and place in the prepared tins. Use a knife to cut four diagonal slashes across the top of each loaf. Brush with melted butter. Bake for 45–50 minutes, until the crust is light brown and the loaf sounds hollow when the base is tapped.

Per portion Energy 1975kcal/8371kJ; Protein 46.1g; Carbohydrate 398.4g, of which sugars 50g; Fat 33.1g, of which saturates 17.4g; Cholesterol 71mg; Calcium 940mg; Fibre 29.3g; Sodium 361mg.

Makes 2 loaves

40g/1½oz fresh yeast

250ml/8fl oz/1 cup buttermilk

40g/1½ oz/3 tbsp butter

120ml/4fl oz/½ cup treacle (molasses)

350g/12oz/3 cups dark rye flour

45ml/3 tbsp caraway seeds

7.5ml/1½ tsp salt

500g/1½ /5 cups unbleached bread flour

15g/½oz/1 tbsp melted butter

Cook's tip Substitute 115g/4oz/1 cup rye meal for the same amount of rye flour to give the bread a coarser texture.

Useful addresses

Australia

www.igourmet.com/australianfood

Scandinavia

ICA ute i världen
(Swedish food specialities such
as caviar, sill, surströmming and
chocolate)
niklas.gloggler@nara.ica.se
www.icasvensktmat.se

The Northerner
(Gifts, food and crafts)
Flöjelbergsgatan 16A
43135 Mölndal, Sweden
Tel: 007 812 272 57 37
www.northerner.com

United Kingdom

Danish Deli Food
Somewhere Ltd.
6-8 Underwood Street
London N1 7JQ
Tel: 45 29 41 24 07
www.danish-deli-food.com

Danish Food Shop
Operated by Bechman Ltd.
Woodbridge
United Kingdom
Tel: 44 (0) 1394 648 198
www.danishfood.net

Danish Food Direct
The Old Coach House
Cranes Yard
Turvey
Bedfordshire MK43 8EN
Tel: 44 (0) 1234 888788
www.DanishFoodDirect.co.uk

Scandelicious
Visit: Scandelicious at
Borough Market
Southwark Street
London SE1 9AB

Contact: Scandelicious
4 Beaconsfield Road
Aldeburgh
Suffolk IP15 5HF
Tel: 01728 452880
www.scandelicious.co.uk

United States

Ingebretsen Scandinavian Foods
1601 East Lake Street
Minneapolis, MN 55407
Tel: 001 (612) 729-9331
www.ingebretsens.com

Larsen Brothers Danish Bakery
8000 24th Ave NW
Seattle, WA 98117
Tel: 001 (206) 782-8285
www.larsenbakery.com

Nielsen's Authentic Danish
Pastries
520 – 2nd Avenue North
Seattle, WA 98119
Tel: 001 (206) 282-3004
www.nielsenspastries.com

Olson's Scandinavian Foods
2248 NW Market St
Seattle, WA 98107
Tel: 001 (206) 783-8288
www.scandinavianfoods.net

The Nordic Heritage Museum
Art Galleries, Immigrant Exhibits,
Museum Shop
3014 NW 67th Street
Seattle, WA 98117
Tel: 001 (206) 789-5707
www.nordicmuseum.net

Scandia Imports
10020 SW Beaverton-Hillsdale
Highway
Beaverton, OR 97005
Tel: 001 (800) 834-8547
www.scandiaimports.com

Scandinavian Specialties
6719 – 15th Avenue NW
Seattle, WA 98177
Tel: 001 (877) 784-7020
001 (206) 784-7020
www.scanspecialties.com

Genuine Scandinavia, LLC.
(Kitchenware, crockery and
accessories)
958 Washington Street, #9
Denver, CO 80203
Tel: 001 (303) 318 0714
Sales@GenuineScandinavia.com
www.GenuineScandinavia.com

The Gift Chalet
(Specializing in everything from
Scandinavia, including food)
8 Washington Street – Route 20
Auburn, MA 01501
Tel: 001 (508) 755-3028
GiftChalet@aol.com
www.giftchaletauburn.com

Nordic Fox
(Restaurant featuring
Scandinavian foods)
10924 Paramount Blvd.
Downey, CA 90241
Phone: 001 (562) 869 1414

Nordic House
3421 Telegraph Avenue
Oakland, CA 94609
Tel: 001 (510) 653-3882
pia@nordichouse.com
www.nordichouse.com

Olson's Delicatessen
(Scandinavian foods and gifts)
5660 West Pico Blvd
Los Angeles, CA
Tel: 001 (323) 938 0742

Scandia Food & Gifts Inc
30 High Street
Norwalk, CT 06851
Tel: 001 (203) 838 2087
scandia@webquill.com
www.scandiafood.com

Scandinavian Marketplace
PO Box 274
218 Second Street East
Hastings, MN 55033
Tel: 1-(800) 797-4319
steve@scandinavianmarket.com
www.scandinavianmarket.com/

Signal Seafoods, Inc.
(Swedish crayfish delivered to all
of North America)
7355 SW 240th Place
Beaverton, OR
Tel: 001 (503) 626 6342
sales@crawfishparty.com
www.crayfishparty.com

IKEA

The international Swedish chain
IKEA has sites in Europe, North
America, the Middle East and
Asia Pacific. Each store has a
Scandinavian food market
stocking specialist ingredients –
from unrefined hard bread to
caviar spread. Check your local
IKEA store by visiting
www.ikea.com

Index

A

agriculture 7, 8
alcohol 19
almonds
  almond ring cake 114
  Danish pastry 122
  mazarins 121
apples 6, 9, 18, 83, 92
  bacon with apples 59
  old-fashioned apple cake 106
aquavit 15, 19
asparagus 10
  tartlets 30

B

bacon 7, 16
  bacon with apples 59
  liver pâté with bacon and
    mushrooms 56
beef 78
  beef patties with onions and
    fried egg 90
  beef tartare with egg yolk,
    onion and beetroot 60
  mock hare, redcurrant jelly
    sauce and Hasselback
    potatoes 84
  roast beef, remoulade, crispy
    onions and horseradish 61
beer 6, 11, 15, 19
  beer soup with whipped
    cream 104
beetroot 7, 17
  pickled beetroot 39
berries 6, 9, 17–18
  red berry soup with cream
    102
bread 6, 7, 15, 18
  dark rye bread 125
butter 7, 15, 17
buttermilk soup 103

C

cabbage 7, 17
  braised red cabbage 38
capers 60

cauliflower soup with prawns 25
caviar with toast and crème
    fraîche 36
cheese 7, 17
cherries 9, 18
  rice pudding with warm cherry
    sauce 108
  venison tenderloins with cherry
    sauce 91
chicken 16, 78
  braised chicken 95
  chicken soup 26
  roast chicken with
    lingonberries 96
Christmas 13
cod 6, 16, 64
  baked cod with cream 68
  salt cod with mustard sauce
    66
Constitution Day 13, 109
cream
  baked cod with cream 68
  beer soup with whipped
    cream 104
  Danish caviar with toast and
    crème fraîche 36
  fried eel with potatoes in
    cream sauce 69
  layer cake with cream and
    raspberries 110
  marinated herring in sour
    cream 48
  National Day dessert 109
  red berry soup with cream
    102

crispbread 18
cucumber 7, 9, 17
  cucumber salad 40
  prawns with egg and
    cucumber 54
currants 17

D

dairy produce 7, 16–17
Denmark 6–7
  cuisine 10–11
  festivals and holidays 12–13
  geography 8–9
  open sandwiches 7, 14–15,
    44, 46–61
  produce 16–19
desserts 100
dill 17, 47, 50
doughnuts Danish-style 113
duck roasted with prunes and
    apples 92
dumplings 26

E

Easter 12
  Easter rack of lamb 88
eel 6, 16, 64
  fried eel with potatoes in
    cream sauce 69
eggs 7, 17
  beef patties with onions and
    fried egg 90
  beef tartare with egg yolk,
    onion and beetroot 60
  cold buttermilk soup 103
  herring in tomato sauce with
    egg and dill 47
  prawns with egg and
    cucumber 54
  smoked salmon with
    scrambled eggs 51

F

Fastelavn 12
fish 6, 7, 9, 16, 64
  fish cakes 74

  shooting star 53
fruit 6, 17–18
  Danish dried fruit soup 105

G

game 16, 78
  venison tenderloins with
    cherry sauce 91

H

halibut 16, 64
  halibut fillets with parsley
    sauce 75
ham with Italian salad 55
herbs 17
herring 6, 16, 64
  fried salt herring with red
    onion compote 72
  herring in tomato sauce with
    egg and dill 47
  herring marinated in sherry 33
  marinated herring in sour
    cream 48
  pickled herring 32
  pickled herring smørrebrød 46
  potatoes with leeks and
    pickled herring 49
hornsalt 19
horseradish 17, 34, 61
  yellow pea soup with
    horseradish cream 24

J

Jerusalem artichokes au gratin
    27

L

lamb 16, 78
  Easter rack of lamb 88
layer cake with cream and
  raspberries 110
leeks 17
  potatoes with leeks and
    pickled herring 49
lemon 50
  lemon marinated salmon with
    horseradish 34
  lemon mousse 107
Lenten buns with vanilla cream
  118
lingonberries 18, 88
  roast chicken with
    lingonberries 96
liver pâté 29, 56

M

marzipan 18, 108
mazarins 121
meat 6, 16, 78
Midsummer Eve 13
Mertensaften 13, 106
mushrooms 9, 18
  liver pâté with bacon and
    mushrooms 56
mustard 9, 19
  salt cod with mustard sauce
    66

N

National Day dessert 109
New Year's Eve 12, 68

O

onions 17, 60, 90
  crispy onion rings 58, 61
  fried salt herring with red onion
    compote 72
open sandwiches 7, 14–15, 44,
  46–61

P

parsley 17
  halibut fillets with parsley
    sauce 75
pastries 7, 18
  Danish pastry 122
pea soup with horseradish

cream 24
plaice 16, 64
  fried plaice fillet with
    remoulade 52
plums 9, 18
  plum cake 117
pork 6, 7, 16, 78
  Danish meatballs 87
  liver pâté 28
  liver pâté with bacon and
    mushrooms 56
  mock hare, redcurrant jelly
    sauce and Hasselback
    potatoes 84
  pork loin stuffed with apples
    and prunes 83
  pork fillet with crispy
    onion rings 58
  roast pork, crackling and
    glazed potatoes 80
  veterinarian's evening
    sandwich 57
potatoes 7, 10, 17, 18
  fried eel with potatoes in
    cream sauce 69
  Hasselback potatoes 84
  potato salad 41
  potatoes with leeks and
    pickled herring 49
  roast pork, crackling and
    glazed potatoes 80
  salmon steaks with warm
    potato salad 71
prawns 16, 64
  cauliflower soup with prawns
    25
  prawns with egg and
    cucumber 54
  tartlets 30
prunes 83, 92

R

raspberries 9, 17, 102
  layer cake with cream and
    raspberries 110
remoulade 52, 61, 68, 74
rhubarb 18
  National Day dessert 109
rice pudding with warm cherry
  sauce 108

S

salmon 6, 16, 64
  lemon-marinated salmon with
    horseradish 34
  salmon steaks with warm
    potato salad 71
  smoked salmon with dill and
    lemon 50
  smoked salmon with
    scrambled eggs 51
seasonings 19
sherry-marinated herring 33
shooting star 53
smørrebrød see open
  sandwiches
spices 19
Store Bededag 12–13
Swiss roll 112

T

tartlets 30

V

Valborgsaften 13
vanilla 19
  Lenten buns with vanilla cream
    118
  vanilla rings 124
veal 78
  Danish meatballs 87
vegetables 9, 17
  Italian salad 55
venison tenderloins with cherry
  sauce 91

W

Whitsun 13

Y

yellow pea soup with
  horseradish cream 24

Author's acknowledgements

I'm the recipient of Danish generosity both at the table and in writing this cookbook, with Danish friends in the US and in Denmark who have opened their hearts and homes to me over the years. My warmest thanks go to Inger Sieffert, Kristine and Klaus Kostending, and Suzanne Hohlen for their enthusiasm and counsel. And it was Zita Røschke of Humlebæk who first introduced me to *lever postej* and the delights of the Danish *koldt bord*. My life changed with my first taste!

I also owe a special thanks to John Nielsen whose explanations, willing availability and expert suggestions were invaluable to compiling the recipes. One taste of his flaky *Viennabrød* and you know you're in the company of a master Danish pastry chef. I was fortunate that he didn't need much persuasion participate in this project, even though retired.

The Anness production team has also earned my applause, its talented stylist Helen Trent, the dedicated food team under Fergel Connelly's direction, and photographer, William Lingwood, who worked together to bring these Danish dishes alive. I also want to thank my brilliant editorial team, Beverley Jollands, who copy edited every recipe backwards and forwards, and project editor, Joanne Rippin, whose patience, enthusiasm, sense of humour and constant grace urged me onward.

Additional images supplied by Art Archive p7t; Corbis pp 7b, 11, 13l, and Bridgeman Art Library p6.